THE NEW PROTECTIONISM
THE WELFARE STATE AND
INTERNATIONAL TRADE

INTERNATIONAL CENTER FOR ECONOMIC POLICY STUDIES BOOKS

The International Center for Economic Policy Studies, a nonprofit, nonpartisan institute, which sponsors studies dealing with economic issues, was founded in 1977. The aim of the Center is to provide readable, though analytical, publications, which improve public understanding of economic problems and the market process and, where possible, suggest solutions. Its studies, which are financed with contributions from individuals, corporations and private foundations, are prepared by members of the academic community, usually economists, who engage in independent research and arrive at their own conclusions about the issues they consider. Thus, while the studies reflect the areas of interest of the Directors, the Staff and the academic advisers to the International Center for Economic Policy Studies, the views they present are entirely those of their authors and do not carry the endorsement of either the Directors or the sponsors of the Center.

THE NEW PROTECTIONISM

THE WELFARE STATE AND INTERNATIONAL TRADE

MELVYN B. KRAUSS
Professor of Economics
New York University

Published by New York University Press
for the
International Center for Economic Policy Studies
1978

Copyright © 1978 by The International Center for Economic Policy Studies

Library of Congress Cataloging in Publication Data

Krauss, Melvyn B
  The new protectionism.

  Includes index.
    1. Free trade and protection—Protection.
2. Welfare state. 3. Commerce. I. Inter-
national Center for Economic Policy Studies.
II. Title.
HF1713.K73   382.7   78-19545
ISBN 0-8147-4570-9
ISBN 0-8147-4571-7 pbk.

Manufactured in the United States of America

CONTENTS

FOREWORD

The first publication of ICEPS is making its appearance at an opportune time. At no period in this century has the body of educated men and women who work seriously with economic and social ideas been more receptive to intelligent alternatives to the conventional wisdom.

The ready solution to every social problem is no longer more and more government intervention or another large scale social program. There is a growing belief among intellectuals and policymakers that government, while well motivated, must be doing something wrong. As more programs are carefully and critically evaluated and judged by their results, rather than by their intentions, this belief will doubtless grow ... until it in turn becomes the conventional wisdom.

Twenty years ago in Great Britain, when the Institute for Economic Affairs was first launched by Antony Fisher, Ralph Harris and Arthur Seldon, almost no one in that

country took much notice. Even a few years ago a
respected editor of a British weekly casually referred to a
pleasant visit he had had with the "lunatics" at IEA. In
Britain today the once derided "lunatics" are taken very
seriously indeed by almost everyone; while all will not
agree on every specific recommendation, all thoughtful
economists and critics of society now know that they must
understand and take into account the documented analyses and arguments of those who prefer the workings of the
market to the machinery of the state.

We were particularly pleased therefore, when an experi-
enced and talented scholar in economics, Dr. Harold M.
Hochman, accepted our invitation to become the first
research director of ICEPS. Under his editorial direction I
know that ICEPS will flourish and will become yet
another font of critiques and alternatives to compete, and
eventually to make its mark, in the market place of ideas.

ICEPS, while newly founded, is also in the fortunate
position of being the beneficiary of the wisdom and
experience of Antony Fisher. For the past twenty years he
has served as the chairman of the board of trustees of the
highly respected IEA in England. Our academic trustee is
Professor David I. Meiselman, Professor of Economics at
the Virginia Polytechnic Institute and State University
and Director of its Graduate Economics Program in
Northern Virginia. David's rigorous work in economics is
well-known to all serious economists.

We are also delighted that the Honorable William J.
Casey and President Joel Segall have agreed to serve on
our Board of Directors. Mr. Casey has also agreed to serve
as Chairman of the Board. Mr. Casey's distinguished
service to the nation as a legal scholar and in high-ranking
government positions gives an important practical dimension to our product. President Segall brings with him his
experience at Baruch College of the City University of

New York and as a distinguished federal official in the Departments of Labor and the Treasury.

Speaking personally, it is an honor for me to work with such distinguished gentlemen and I look forward to a long and fruitful association with the Board and scholars of ICEPS.

Edwin J. Feulner, Jr.
President of the Board of Directors
International Center for Economic Policy Studies
August 1978

INTRODUCTION

The basic defense of free trade, to which subsequent generations have contributed but marginal improvement, can be traced to *The Wealth of Nations.* There are, indeed, few concepts so revered in economic tradition, quite independent of ideology, as free trade. It seems fitting, therefore, that the International Center for Economic Policy Studies, which is founded on the conviction that free markets are essential to human welfare, has chosen "the new protectionism" as the topic of its initial publication.

To many of us, it is a signal disappointment that the emerging liberal order, reflected in the Kennedy round of tariff reductions of the 1960's, appears to have been superseded by a wave of neo-mercantilist restriction, notwithstanding the current efforts of the Tokyo Round of trade negotiations. Non-tariff barriers to trade, more insidious in their effect than tariffs because they do not work through the price mechanism, have proliferated, taking a variety of forms, in violation of the spirit if not the letter of the international understanding on which the General Agreement on Tariffs and Trade is founded. The increase in non-tariff restriction is all the more paradoxical because it has occurred despite significant positive change in the international monetary order, which has brought, in the main, exchange rate flexibility, and freed domestic economic policies from their prior dependence on balance of payments considerations.

In this volume, written for the International Center for Economic Policy Studies, Professor Melvyn Krauss of New York University, with care and significant insight, traces the roots and the effects of the new protectionism. The core of the argument is that non-tariff protection differs, in both structure and form, from the tariff protection to which the Kennedy round was directed. Its heart is the thesis that the new forms of intervention, which protect *specific industries* and *specific segments of the labor force*, are associated with the interventionist or welfare state and are, indeed, an integral and inevitable by-product of the social process that produces it. In a welfare state, Krauss argues, the raison d'etre of government intervention into the private economy is to provide economic security, by shielding citizens from changes that would affect them adversely *and*, in general, redistributing income and economic power from capital to labor. To satisfy these objectives, if indeed they can be satisfied, the role of government is expanded, an effect fully consistent with the private bureaucratic objectives of the civil servants and politicians who are charged with the legislative and administrative responsibilities of governance. Where the immediate costs of welfare state policies are imposed, or appear to rest, on foreigners (who are, by definition not represented in the home country electorate) resistance to this process is minimized.

It is from this interpretation of the implications of welfare state policies for international trade that Krauss ultimately derives his major conclusions, that the welfare state suffers from an inner contradiction, because it both depends upon economic growth for support and, at the same time, reduces it through practices that are inimical to economic efficiency. In a sense, then, Krauss turns the Marxist argument on its head. Though "economic growth may permit social consumption in the short run," he points out, "the true relationship between economic growth and social consumption is competitive—that is, there exists . . . a 'trade-off' between economic growth and social consumption." High levels of social consumption "necessarily imply protectionist measures that stagnate the economy." The heart of the problem is with the demand for "social policies that promise economic security"—that keep labor and capital in low productivity uses where they are comfortable instead of forcing their adjustment to alternative high productivity activities. The effect is an economy that protects its weak industries, through extensive intervention into the private economy and the adoption of protectionist devices, and is prevented, by social commitments, from adjusting to constant environmental changes. The consequence is stagnation, attributable to the inflexibility and the rigidity that inhere in the interventionist state and in the desire for "cradle to grave" economic security to which it gives substance.

Thus, Krauss argues that "the demand for secure economic income at a given level . . . regardless of the changes that are being wrought elsewhere, proves illusory, because the attempt to obtain the secure income [in breaking the link between production and consumption] reduces the ability of the economy to continue to produce it." In the long run, economic progress is incompatible with the reduction of competitive incentives that welfare state intervention entails.

In developing his thesis, Krauss presents a clear and, so far as is possible, non-technical discussion of the subject of international trade. Coupled with his primary theme, the relationship between the welfare state and international trade, this discussion of trade theory and trade policy enhances the appeal of this book for classroom use. To lay the foundation for the broader argument, the initial chapter discusses the alternatives of free trade and protectionism in a competitive context and develops the standard argument for free trade, as seen from a world viewpoint. It makes clear, however, that price distortions through tariffs are to be preferred to non-price intervention, should countries choose to intervene in trade. Krauss then discusses the international trade effects of a wide variety of welfare state interventions and deals with the problems of global harmonization—the difficulties of maintaining the integrity of both welfare state and free market economies when they are linked by international exchange. His conclusion, which follows, focuses on the inherent contradiction of the welfare state, as discussed in the preceding paragraphs.

Though there are points at which any reader may legitimately disagree with the author, there can be little question that the overall argument, as Krauss presents it here, rings true. Ultimately, his lesson is one we should long since have learned—that there is not only no Utopia in which incomes are secure and risk non-existent, but the effort to effect a Utopian existence, through government intervention in private markets, may be welfare-reducing rather than welfare-increasing. Nor is this effect, in any sense, strictly aggregative. In large measure, the welfare effects of the new protectionism are distributive, with some groups (including politicians) capturing benefits at the expense of the community-at-large. In the final analysis, it is the long-term dynamic effects—the economic stagnation that results from the failure of too many modern politicians (as well as their economic advisers) to read the lessons of Adam Smith with the care they deserve—that are most dangerous.

It is our hope that this book, the first the International Center for Economic Policy Studies has produced, can attain a wide audience among both laymen and students of the modern economy. Our intention is to provide readable material that enhances general knowledge of economic problems and the implications of economic policy. In scope, the program ICEPS has designed, with the support, as of this date, of more than thirty different individuals and organizations, is quite broad, though to begin with it has emphasized two substantive areas— international economic policy and the problems of urban communities. There is an important sense in which these two areas are not nearly so different as they may appear, for urban areas, if anything, are prototypes of the open economy that is central to the basic analysis of international trade. In general, the thrust of our studies is not a naive demand for a return to laissez faire, with simple minimization of government activity, but a desire to increase the recognition, by non-economists, that markets, unless there exist compelling arguments to the contrary, are preferable to administrative processes as channels of resource allocation.

In this initial product of the International Center for Economic Policy Studies, it is appropriate to give thanks to all of the parties, individual or corporate, whose support has made it possible for us to begin operations and to achieve what we have in a period of less than a year. There are, however, two people who deserve special mention. One is our Executive Director, Mr. Antony G. A. Fisher, who has brought to ICEPS the experience and wisdom that he has accumulated since, a quarter century ago, as a British businessman with a passionate interest in economic issues, he initiated the Institute for Economic Affairs in London. The other is Mrs. Lynne Middelveen, our Office Manager, who has taken a formal corporate charter and turned ICEPS into an active and functioning organization at the expense of far more effort and time than she would have dared to commit when Antony Fisher first talked her into joining the organization. It is also proper, I believe, to thank the author himself, Professor Melvyn Krauss. In his ability to deliver a high-quality manuscript on time, he has been an ideal author, well worth the lessons in bargaining to which he has subjected me.

We hope that those of you who have occasion to read this book find it not only stimulating but useful. We welcome your comments and any suggestions you may have of directions in which ICEPS might turn. The International Center exists, after all, not for our benefit, but yours, because the maintenance of a society in which public policy is proper is in the interest of us all.

> Harold M. Hochman
> Research Director
> International Center for Economic Policy Studies

July, 1978

PREFACE

The 1960s were great years for free traders. The Kennedy Round of trade negotiations reduced tariffs to unprecedented low levels, and there were hopes that the world economy was on the brink of a truly liberal international economic order. These hopes have been dashed, most decidedly, by the experience of the 1970s. The Tokyo Round of trade negotiations, to remove the so-called nontariff barriers to trade (NTBs), has not gotten past stage one, and instead there has been a marked increase in protectionism in the industrialized states.

The *Wall Street Journal* of April 14, 1978, in an article entitled "Surge in Protectionism Worries and Perplexes Leaders of Many Lands," states: "After three decades of immense increase in world trade and living standards, exports and imports are causing tense pressures in nearly every nation and among the best of allies. The U.S. sets

price floors against Japanese steel, Europe accuses the U.S.
of undercutting its papermakers, the Japanese decry cheap
textiles from South Korea, French farmers have smashed
truckloads of Italian wine, and AFL-CIO President
George Meany rattles exporters world-wide by calling free
trade—'a joke'—"

The tide appears to have turned against free traders. In
their eternal struggle with protectionists, who dominates,
according to the common wisdom, is said to depend upon
the state of general economic conditions. Free traders hold
sway in periods of economic prosperity, and protectionists
dominate when the economy is depressed. The 1960s were
good years; hence we had free or, at least, freer trade. The
1970s have not been such good years; thus, protectionists
currently hold forth.

If one subscribes to this interpretation of events, the
term "new protectionism" simply means the *latest* out-
break of protectionism. But the term can be given a
different interpretation that perhaps better explains its
current widespread use. This is to interpret the word
"new" as "different in structure or form," not as "latest";
hence, the "new protectionism" implies that there has
been a dramatic change on the world scene; that some new
entity is with us that has not been there before. This new
entity, I submit, is the interventionist, or welfare, state.

The welfare state can be defined as a non-communist
egalitarian state in which substantial government intervention in economic and social affairs is accepted as normal.
Its development has been most complete in Scandinavia
and the Netherlands. But one can find welfare-state-type
interventions in all countries, even those that are ide-
ologically committed to the free enterprise market
economy.

Government interventions into the private economy are
the lifeblood of the welfare state. The raison d'être of

these interventions is: (1) to provide economic security for its citizens by protecting them from change that would adversely affect their economic positions; and (2) to redistribute income (and economic power in general) from capital to labor. In practice, these two objectives often come to the same thing.

The growth of welfare state policies since the end of World War II, in both the so-called welfare states and the rest of the industrialized world, has been striking. This growth has meant an increase in the number of "target variables" that governments hope to achieve. For example, no longer do governments aim only for full employment; they also aim for satisfactory *distributions* of employment among regions, sexes, and races. The new protectionism is not a recent occurrence of an old phenomenon; it reflects new attitudes toward the proper role of government in the economy.

To some extent, these new attitudes toward the proper role of government have been the result—intended or otherwise—of the competition of politicians for public office in democracies. One politician tries to outdo the other in making promises to the electorate, and the electorate comes to think of these promises as something that a good government *should* be doing for them—that is, as legitimate functions of government. This situation, of course, is very convenient for the politicians for, as Jan Tumlir points out, each promise entails a function for the government, so that the overall effect is for the "governments to be soliciting additional functions for themselves." The greater the number of functions, the greater the economic power of the politician.

If the new protectionism is a consequence of the emergence of the welfare state for international trade—and the trend toward the welfare state has gone on, more or less, since the end of World War II, how can one explain the tariff-cutting Kennedy Round? One explanation consistent with the above hypothesis is that the Kennedy Round represented a situation in which protectionists in fact gave away very little while free traders thought they had gained a lot. The hallmark of welfare state interventionism is that it is selective and fine-tuned to specific problems. The tariff is a clumsy instrument for many purposes, unable to distinguish among different regions, different social groups, different firms, and so on. To give up the tariff was for the welfare states a "cheap" way to improve their internationalist credentials. The Kennedy Round can thus be interpreted as an exchange between free traders and protectionists from which both parties gained but which did not alter the basic course of the world economy toward increased interventionism.

The Welfare State and International Trade

The increased incidence of welfare state policies in the industrialized nations and in international trade is related in two ways. One might ask how the welfare state policies themselves affect international trade, or how the existence of international trade affects the ability of domestic policymakers to effectuate welfare state policies. An example of the former is the effect of regional policies on a country's imports and exports. An example of the latter is the effect of "guest workers" (imported labor) on a country's ability to redistribute income from capital to labor.

The relation between the welfare state and international trade is the central theme of this book. The theme is pursued on several different levels. First, there are questions of the type mentioned in the preceding paragraph. Emphasis is on welfare state *policies* rather than on the welfare state as a structural unit or entity. The analysis here often is as relevant to the United States and West Germany as it is to Sweden and Norway. Second, there are questions that relate to the coexistence of welfare state and free market economies engaged in international exchange. The essential problem is that the linkage of the two types of economies, through international trade, can threaten the "integrity" of each "economic system."

Finally, the book explores the question of stagnation and the welfare state. It is argued that the welfare state both depends upon economic growth to support it and reduces economic growth. Thus, it suffers from its own "inner contradiction." This argument has obvious implications for the malaise affecting the Organization for Economic Cooperation and Development (OECD) economies during the 1970s. The increased demand for economic security may be inducing an amount of inflexibility and immobility into the Western industrialized economies that prevents them from growing.

Outline

The specific outline of the book is simple. To establish the ground for the discussion of policy, the first chapter considers the traditional issue of free trade and protectionism in the context of a competitive economy. It is argued that the conflict between the economic interests of specific groups within the community and the economic interests of the community as a whole is the essence of the issue of free trade versus protectionism. The second chapter compares the new and the old protectionism and quickly introduces the main theme of the book: the relationship between the welfare state and international trade. Chapter III considers a variety of interventionist policies and the effect they have on international trade. Examples of such policies are domestic subsidies, export subsidies, environmental measures, adjustment assistance, income transfer policies, and so on. There is also an analysis of the effect that income transfers from capital to labor have on "capital flight" and "guest workers." Chapter IV is concerned with the problem of world tax and subsidy harmonization, that is, the problem of maintaining the "integrity" of both welfare state and free market economies, each with different tax and subsidy policies, when they are linked by international exchange. Finally, the theme of stagnation and the welfare state is taken up in Chapter V, and the inherent contradictions of the welfare state are explored.

CHAPTER I

FREE TRADE VERSUS PROTECTIONISM

One of the several issues in economics that always appears to be with us is that of free trade versus protectionism. It is also an issue extremely relevant to the main theme of this book—protectionism and the welfare state.

Free trade as an objective of international commercial policy can be, and indeed has been, supported from a variety of different standpoints. Some statesmen have advocated free trade as the best policy for avoiding international disputes. Protectionism in one country can lead to protectionism in another, with economic questions developing unhealthy political and military overtones. The classical economic argument for free trade, however, is not based on this laudable goal but on the perhaps equally laudable one of efficiency in the allocation of the world's economic resources. After all, waste by one means is not inherently superior to waste by any other.

The Argument for Foreign Trade

The essential argument for foreign trade set forth by the classical economists is easy to comprehend: given a fixed stock of productive resources, free trade permits the *consumption* possibilities available to the economy to expand beyond the economy's *production* possibilities. In an isolated economy (in other words, an economy that does not trade), domestic consumption is limited to production. But through international trade, it is possible for the economy's consumption of all goods to increase beyond the its ability to produce these goods.

In Figure 1 a simple diagram illustrates the so-called gains from international trade. Consider an economy that can produce only two goods—pickles and ice cream. Given the economy's supply of land, labor, capital, and the state of its technical skill, the curve *PP* represents the maximum amount of one good that the economy can produce for given amounts of the other good. The basic law of scarcity is reflected by the fact that *PP* falls from the upper left to the lower right. To produce increasing amounts of one good, the output of the other must be reduced.

In an isolated economy, *PP* defines both the economy's production and consumption alternatives, assuming full employment. Consumption at points *A′* and *A″*, for example, clearly lie outside the economy's capabilities. They can be reached only if the economy grows; that is, the curve *PP* shifts outward because of, say, technical progress. However, if the economy has the opportunity to trade at the price ratio given by the slope of *CC* (the slope

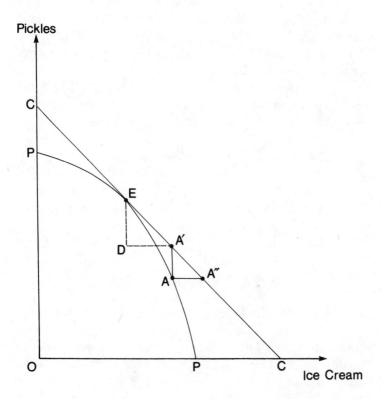

FIGURE 1.

of *CC* shows how many units of pickles exchange for a unit of ice cream in the world market), consumption along the line *CC* is possible if domestic production is adjusted to point *E*. The consumption alternatives available to the economy have expanded from *PEP* to *CEC*, even though the production possibility curve has not altered.

Assume initially that the economy produces and consumes the combination of goods indicated at point *A*. Given the opportunity to trade at the international price ratio indicated by the slope of *CC*, if production shifts to point *E*, consumption at point *A'* is possible. The economy exports *ED* amount of pickles and, at the given world price, receives *DA'* amount of ice cream in return. Indeed all points on *CC* are possible via international trade, including those that lie between *A'* and *A"*. All points between *A'* and *A"* of course, represent increased consumption of both goods by comparison with the initial isolated-economy point *A*. This is the essential argument for international trade.

The Heckscher-Ohlin Theory

The reason cited most often by economists for the existence of the "gains from international trade" is the so-called Heckscher-Ohlin theory. Both Eli Heckscher and his student Bertil Ohlin argued that there were likely to be systematic differences in the ratio of factors of production found in different countries. One country will have an abundance of labor relative to its supply of land, and the opposite will be true in other countries. At the same time, it could be expected that technology between goods would be different in the sense that at given prices for the factors of production, efficient production of some commodities would require a high ratio of labor to land, while efficient production of other commodities would require a high ratio of land to labor. The fundamental idea is that, both for the world as a whole and its constituent nations, it is more efficient for each country to concentrate on the commodity that uses its relatively abundant factor intensively in its production and to import the other good than for each country to attempt to produce large amounts of both goods. The labor-abundant country should concentrate its production on the labor-intensive good and import the land-intensive good, and vice versa for the land-abundant country. In other words, the gains from international trade result from the correct matching of land-intensive and labor-intensive production technologies of goods with different factor supply or endowment ratios between countries.

An Attack on Mercantilism

The argument for free trade was developed to criticize the mercantilistic practices of governments in the eighteenth century. The mercantilists identified a nation's wealth or well-being with its stock of precious metals. Accordingly, a country was encouraged to export more than it imported, since the *net* outflow of goods would be matched by an inflow of gold. To stimulate a "favorable" balance of trade, tariffs and export subsidies often were resorted to. The tariff discouraged imports, while the export subsidy encouraged exports.

The thrust of the "classical" attack on mercantilism by Adam Smith, in particular, was that the mercantilists misspecified the "wealth of nations" by identifying it with its stock of precious metals rather than with the consumption alternatives available to the nation's citizens. While tariffs and export subsidies could increase the nation's (i.e., the government's) stock of precious metals, they would also simultaneously reduce the economy's consumption alternatives by comparison with a policy of free trade. The classical economists argued that the latter constituted a decrease in the real wealth of the nation, even though the government's gold stock would be increased by trade interventions. Free trade is a better policy if the intent is to maximize a country's consumption opportunities.

The Public versus Special Interest

The classical argument for free trade is an argument based on the overall or aggregate (of groups) economic well-being of the society. Free trade is best for the overall economy, even though individual groups may lose from this policy. In essence, the classical argument against mercantilism is an argument of this kind. Even though one of the groups within the economy—the government—may gain from the imposition of tariffs and export subsidies, the overall economy loses by it.

The conflict between the economic interests of specific groups within the community and the economic interests of the community as a whole is the essence of the free trade versus protectionism controversy. Free traders argue from the standpoint of the overall economy; protectionists argue from the standpoint of particular interest groups. Nowhere is this conflict more apparent than in the analysis of the tariff.

The Economics of the Tariff

The tariff is a tax on imports that, at given world prices, raises the internal, or domestic, price of the import good in proportion to the rate at which the tariff is imposed. This means that domestic consumers must pay a higher price for the import good and that domestic producers of import substitutes receive a higher price for their output than would be the case were free trade pursued.

If the economy is divided into three groups—domestic consumers of the import good, domestic producers of import substitutes, and the government—it is clear that domestic consumers lose, domestic producers gain, and the government gains (tariff revenue) from the tariff. At first glance, it might seem that the tariff is a good thing because two groups gain and one loses. But it can be easily shown that the *amount* domestic consumers lose is necessarily greater than the *sum* of the gains of domestic producers and the government. Hence, if the society values each economic actor equally—that is, if a dollar's gain for domestic producers is equal to a dollar's gain for domestic consumers and a dollar's gain for government, the tariff can be said to reduce the economy's overall economic well-being (see Appendix A to this chapter).

The reason for this result is easy to understand. The imposition of the tariff has two types of effects. One may be called a distributional, or an income transfer effect; the other, a resource allocation effect. The income transfer effect refers to the fact that by increasing the domestic price of imports by comparison with their levels under free trade, the tariff causes income to be redistributed among groups in the community. The resource allocation effect refers to the fact that the tariff induces inefficient levels of both the production and the consumption of import substitutes. The tariff induces too much domestic production of the import good and too little consumption of it.

What too much domestic production of import substitutes means is that, given the world price of these goods, it is cheaper for the country to import the *additional* domestic output of import substitutes induced by the tariff than to produce it at home. What too little domestic consumption of the import good means is that the tariff encourages a less than socially optimal level of domestic consumption of the import good. That is, with the tariff, the benefit to the community from an additional unit of consumption of the import good is greater than the import cost of the additional unit to the community. But the additional unit of the good will not be imported because the tariff has made its cost to consumers artificially too expensive.

Assume that the object of government policy is to transfer income to domestic producers of import substitutes. Hence, it is only the income transfer effect of the tariff that is desired. But one cannot have one effect of the tariff without the other. The resource allocation effect, which reduces overall economic well-being by inducing a misallocation of resources, comes along with the income transfer effect. This is why the overall community loses from the income transfer when the latter is effectuated by the tariff. Ideally, the income transfer should be made without the resource allocation effect, but this is not possible when the tariff is the redistribution mechanism.

The argument that income transfers between groups in the economy should be effectuated "outside the marketplace"—that is, should not be made by distorting prices in the marketplace—is based precisely on the above argumentation. When prices are adjusted to transfer incomes, resource misallocation comes along with the income transfer—unless, of course, prices were not "correct" to begin with. But even in this case it would be highly fortuitous if the price change required to effectuate the income transfer were the precise price correction needed for efficient resource allocation. In general, it is a good rule of thumb that market prices not be manipulated to redistribute incomes when such redistribution is decided upon by community consensus.

Hidden Redistribution

The fact of the matter, though, is that tariffs and other protectionist devices are often used to redistribute income within the economy precisely because no such consensus exists in the body politic and that redistribution by the tariff is less obvious than other means the government can employ. Thus, the tariff is often used to redistribute incomes when the government wants to hide the income transfer. This kind of device is used when the redistribution has little to do with accepted standards of distributional equity in the economy but amounts, more or less, to a "payoff" to particular groups for some reason.

Consider the case of shoe manufacturers in the United States. There is no evidence of community consensus that distributional equity requires an increase in the real incomes of U.S. shoe manufacturers by comparison with other groups. Yet the Carter administration has been eager to transfer income to this group and has done so by imposing import restrictions on foreign-made shoes. Undoubtedly *open* redistribution *via* lump-sum subsidies from the public Treasury to shoe manufacturers would have been highly controversial. But redistribution *via* the tariff is *hidden* redistribution: the public may not realize that the higher price of shoes is related to an act of the government; and even if it does realize this, the protection is often justified, not in terms of helping out "friends" of the administration, but as necessary protection against unfair trading practices of foreigners. "Unfair foreign trading practices," as a slogan, appears to have enough xenophobic appeal to make restrictions on international trade a favored way for politicians to redistribute incomes *within* the economy.

For example, the campaign in the United States by the steel industry to receive protection—that is, income transfers from other Americans—that commenced in earnest in 1977 has been fueled in the public press by the slogan that the steel industry believes in *fair* trade if not free trade. This puts the blame for the recent poor performance of the U.S. steel industry squarely on the shoulders of the foreigner; that is, on the "tricks foreigners play" rather than on the "tricks" that the steel industry—unions and management alike—have been playing on the American public for too long a time. That labor costs in the U.S. steel industry have skyrocketed over the past decade cannot be denied. But so long as the higher costs could be passed forward to the consumers without much loss of sales, profits and employment could be protected. The absence of vigorous international competition, in other words, has enabled wages to grow faster than productivity, because neither labor nor management has had sufficient incentive to stop it.

However, years of rising labor costs in the United States in combination with the emergence of the Far Eastern economies as efficient producers of steel and steel products has put the American steel industry on the spot. Either wage increases must be adjusted to productivity gains or profits will be squeezed. Free imports thus force management to keep wage claims in line with productivity gains and, at the same time, restrain excessive profits for capital.

Naturally, if labor and capital employed in the steel industry can convince the U.S. government to give it protection by one means or another, their little game— played at the expense of the rest of the community—can continue. Wages can continue to be higher than productivity improvements, and profits can be unnecessarily high. Moreover, protection today is certain to lead to *increased* protection tomorrow, since the gap between labor costs in the United States and in its foreign competitors can be expected to widen. Without imports to "protect" them, American consumers of steel products will be at the mercy of the steel companies and their organized workers.

The Optimal Tariff Argument

The argument of this chapter is concerned with the tariff as a protective device rather than as a tool to improve the bargaining position of the tariff-imposing country vis-à-vis other countries. Of course, if a country is small in international markets there is little scope for it to reduce the price of its imports by use of a tariff. But a large country is a "price maker" rather than a "price taker," so that a tariff can improve its terms of trade.

The tariff distorts resource allocation within the economy regardless of whether a country is large or small in international markets. But because a tariff imposed by a large country can improve the tariff-imposing country's terms of trade with foreign countries, it is possible for the tariff to improve domestic economic welfare in a large country. In fact, if imposed at a correct rate, it can be rigorously proved that the tariff *must* improve overall domestic welfare. Hence the term "optimal tariff."

But just as a tariff is an inefficient means for effecting internal income redistribution, the tariff can be shown to be an inefficient tool for redistributing income among countries from the point of view of the *world's* economic welfare. It can also lead to retaliation by foreign countries, which can leave the domestic country worse off than if it maintained a free trade policy. Finally, while in the case of the large country the optimal tariff certainly exists, it is questionable whether the government can identify it. The tariff actually imposed by the government can be too high or too low. The optimal tariff is an interesting conception in economic theory, but how much commercial policy in the real world can be explained by it is another matter.

The Tariff as a Tax

It is sometimes forgotten that a tariff is a tax and, as such, can raise revenue to finance government expenditure. Tariffs are not important sources of revenue in developed countries, but they have been important in less developed countries.

Ideally a tax should be imposed in such a way that the loss of real income by the private community is exactly equal to the tax revenue gained by the collective authority. But if the tax distorts prices in the process of affecting the real resource transfer to government, the loss imposed upon the private community will be greater than the tax revenue gained by the government. In the public finance literature, the excess of loss by the private community over tax revenue collected is called the tax's excess burden.

Although the tariff is not an important source of public revenues in developed economies, the fact that the tariff increases rather than decreases tax revenues can be an important reason for using the tariff to achieve *nonrevenue* objectives, such as internal income redistribution. The tariff revenue gains obtained from achieving a nonrevenue objective can be a beneficial side effect for the government.

For example, if the tariff is used to redistribute income to shoe manufacturers in this country, the government gains tax revenue. On the other hand, if the redistribution is made by a production subsidy, the government loses tax revenue. From the point of view of the government, the tariff is thus the preferable vehicle to effectuate the income transfer. However, the production subsidy is more efficient (a formal proof is provided in Appendix B to this chapter). This is because the tariff distorts both production decisions and consumption decisions, while the production subsidy distorts only production decisions.

Since the government is responsible for the mechanism to be used to redistribute incomes internally and it has a vested interest in choosing the mechanism that is less efficient, the tax revenue aspects of the tariff can be an important source of inefficiency in the developed economies, even though tariff revenue is small in proportion to the total tax revenues. There is at least one case where the tax revenue aspects of redistribution have been important in determining the intervention mechanism, and that is in the Common Agricultural Policy of the European Economic Community (EEC). The tariff is used to redistribute income to farmers in the EEC, with the consequent tariff revenue financing certain EEC projects that would not be financed by the individual national governments; that is, the budgets for certain EEC activities depend exclusively on the tariff revenues.

The Tariff versus the Quota

Even free traders recognize that in the battle between a special interest and the general or public interest—the essence of the free trade versus protectionist issue—the special interest sometimes will emerge victorious. In these cases, free traders argue that protection by the tariff is better than its prime alternative, the quota. The tariff is preferred to quota restrictions not only because it is felt to offer more limited protection but, perhaps even more important, because the tariff is felt to be more consistent with the workings of a market economy.

This latter point has been put most forcefully by Gottfried Haberler in his League of Nations study, where he described quota restrictions as being cancerous to the basic foundations of a market economy. Professor Haberler writes: "Quantitative restrictions constitute a much more serious interference with the individualist economy based on the price mechanism and free enterprise than the other type of regulation. We may characterize them as a 'non-conformable' type of interference, a foreign substance, as it were, in the body of the free economy which necessarily leads to dangerous ulcerations and threatens to weaken or undermine the individualist economy altogether. On the other hand, custom tariffs, even high ones, are 'conformable interferences' which do not destroy the price mechanism on the functioning of which a private economy must depend." [1]

The attitude of free traders toward tariffs and quotas thus reflects a second, though closely related, dimension of the free trade versus protectionism issue, in addition to special versus public interest—the issue of the market economy versus the centrally planned economy. Free traders support the market economy because they feel the *public* interest is best served by this type of economic organization. On the other hand, being the standard-bearers of special interest, protectionists seek to change the outcomes that result from the free interaction of buyers and sellers in the marketplace in their favor.

Though protectionists, by necessity, are interventionists, it would be a misinterpretation to suggest that they are ideological advocates of centrally planned economies. Indeed, many protectionists may be staunch defenders of the free market until their own special interest is involved. The logical implication of protectionism, however, is that there be a strong central government that overlooks and intervenes in the marketplace whenever necessary. Given the interventionist government, the full-fledged centrally planned economy may not be far behind. This sequence is by no means compulsory: the interventionist state need not lead to a centrally planned economy. But free traders argue that the danger of this occurring increases if the vehicle of protection takes the form of direct controls (quantitative restrictions) rather than market-price manipulation (the tariff). This explains the often observed fervor of free traders in opposing protection; it is not only the public interest they are defending but the market economy itself.

The argument is sometimes made that the free traders' preference for the tariff compared with the quota as an interventionist vehicle is misplaced. This is the argument that the tariff and the quota are equivalent. However, in one case, the government *declares* that imports will be limited to certain amounts, and domestic prices will adjust accordingly. In the other, prices in the domestic market are manipulated to insure that domestic buyers and sellers "freely" choose to import the precise quantity of goods the government prefers. True restriction on individual freedom is more direct with the quantitative restriction. But the so-called freedom of choice with the tariff is illusory—it is the freedom of the puppet.

The equivalence argument, though attractive, is at variance with the observed behavior of both protectionists and free traders. Protectionists like quotas, and free traders would rather have tariffs—and this is not because both sides are too foolish to see the truth!

One reason why protectionists prefer quotas to tariffs relates to their "elasticity pessimism." [2] Elasticity is a gilt-edged word that economists like to use as a synonym for responsiveness. Protectionists fears that increasing the domestic price of imports will not significantly affect domestic consumption and domestic production of imports—that the demand and supply price elasticities are low. They argue that the tariff rate required to induce (nonresponsive) domestic consumers and producers to "freely" choose the level of imports desired by the protectionists is so astronomically high that politically it could never be approved. The quota, on the other hand, could be sold, since its protective effect is not so obvious. Thus, the tariff and the quota are not equivalent, since the restrictiveness of the tariff is much more obvious than the quota, given the factor of "elasticity pessimism." Of course, if protectionists were "elasticity optimists," the argument would cut the other way—the tariff would be preferred by protectionists. It would be easy to sell an innocuous-looking tariff, and worthwhile to boot, since protectionists would receive a significant protective effect from it.

A second reason why protectionists prefer quotas to tariffs is that a fixed quota provides continuing protection. The rate of protection automatically adjusts to changes in demand and/or supply conditions, whereas a fixed tariff rate provides "one-shot" protection. After the tariff rate is fixed and the initial protective impact felt, the market reacts to demand and/or supply condition changes more or less as it would under free trade—an important difference.

Consider the case of an industry where domestic costs are rising because wage gains are greater than productivity increases—a typical client for protection. If in fact protection is rendered by a fixed rate tariff, as domestic supply decreases, domestic prices do not change by comparison with their initial (distorted) level. Imports increase in proportion to the decrease in domestic supply: this is, more or less, the free trade result, except that with free trade the domestic price level would be lower, the absolute domestic consumption level higher, and absolute domestic production level less than with the tariff.

With a fixed quota the result is different. With the quota, at the initial level of domestic prices the decrease in domestic supply creates a situation where the demand for imports is greater than the quota allowances. The price of the quota allowances therefore is bid up and, with it, the price that domestic consumers are willing to pay and the price that domestic producers receive for the import good. Internal prices rise until the demand for imports once again is equated with the fixed supply of import quota allowances. The rate of protection—the difference between the domestic and world price over the world price—*automatically* has adjusted to the conditions of reduced domestic supply brought about by the fact that the wage gains continue to exceed productivity increases in the domestic industry. Thus, when protection is provided by a fixed quota, there is no operative mechanism to bring wage claims into line with productivity advances.

To sum up, protectionists prefer protection by a quota both because of elasticity pessimism and because with the fixed quota there is an automatic adjustment of the rate of protection to changed conditions of domestic supply and/ or domestic demand. Free traders, on the other hand, prefer the tariff because they tend to be elasticity optimists and because with a fixed tariff the market works more or less as it would under free trade, except that the levels of domestic consumption and production are distorted. In addition, free traders worry about the effect that direct controls have on the "integrity" of the market economy. Judging from the rules that were adopted by the industrial countries to guide their commercial relations with one another after World War II, free traders have been successful in convincing governments of the justness of their cause.

The General Agreement on Tariffs and Trade

The rules or guidelines for conducting international commercial relations among the developed countries after World War II are codified in the General Agreement on Tariffs and Trade (GATT). GATT represents fairly closely the views of the Americans after World War II. The efficacy of the market economy and thus free trade are its basic underlying tenets. If trade is to be restricted, it should be restricted by a tariff; that is, the tariff is the preferred means of trade control. Furthermore, when imposed, tariffs should be on a geographically non-discriminatory basis. This is the *most favored nation* clause of GATT. The tariff rates offered to the most favored nation should be offered to all.

Two exceptions to the most favored nation clause are permitted in GATT. They are: (1) the customs union and (2) the free trade area. The customs union is an institutional arrangement in which members do not impose tariffs on trade with other members but all members impose a common tariff vis-à-vis nonmembers. The free trade area is similar to the customs union except that there is no requirement for a common external tariff vis-à-vis nonmembers. Each party is free to tariff nonmember goods at the rate of its choice.

It may seem strange in this age of U.S. balance-of-payments difficulties that the United States would give its blessing to what in effect would be institutionalized discrimination against its own products. But it did so, and the reason is not hard to find. It was decided by leaders on both sides of the Atlantic that the economic reconstruction of Western Europe would take place within the context of a regional grouping—the European Economic Community. To the United States, getting Western

Europe back on its feet appeared to be worth its economic cost, in terms of institutionalized discrimination against U.S. goods. The regional approach was favored because of the devastating effect nationalism had had in provoking two major wars in that part of the globe.

The Customs Union Issue

Given the fact that Western Europe was to have a customs union, the question arose as to whether a customs union in its pure form represented a move toward free trade or toward greater protectionism. The answer was given by Jacob Viner in his celebrated book, *The Customs Union Issue.*[3]

Viner argued that the effect of a customs union on efficiency in the allocation of resources is ambiguous; this is because a customs union provokes, at the same time, a movement toward freer trade *and* a movement toward increased protection. Domestic producers find their protection eliminated vis-à-vis producers of substitute goods in *partner countries.* This situation is good because it means that the location of production will shift from a high-cost domestic source to a lower-cost partner source. Viner called this effect *trade creation* because the substitution of partner for domestic production implies an increase in imports into the domestic country.

But while the customs union's trade-creation effect increases economic well-being in the domestic country, trade diversion reduces it. *Trade diversion* refers to the fact that the customs union can induce a shift in the location of production from a low-cost nonmember source to a high-cost partner source. This shift can be brought about because partner goods are now protected vis-à-vis nonmember goods in the domestic market as well as in the partner market. If the subsequent tariff disadvantage suffered by nonmember goods vis-à-vis partner substitutes *in the domestic market* is greater than the cost advantage enjoyed by nonmember goods in comparison with their partner counterparts, domestic consumers will switch their imports from the nonmember country to the partner country. Trade will be diverted, and the economic well-being of the domestic country will be reduced as a result.

Trade diversion can be illustrated by a simple arithmetical example. Assume that apples can be obtained at $5 per ton on world markets but at $10 per ton in the partner country (the quality of the apples being the same). There are no domestic apple growers in the domestic market. The cost advantage enjoyed by nonmember producers is $5 per ton, and if there is a tariff that is geographically nondiscriminatory, or no tariff before the customs union is formed, the home country imports apples from nonmembers.

Next, assume that the customs union requires the domestic country to put a $6 per ton tariff on apple imports from non-members but that apple imports from partners enter the domestic market duty-free. Thus, while the non-member continues to enjoy a $5 per ton cost advantage, he now suffers from a $6 per ton tariff disadvantage vis-à-vis partner competition in the domestic market. Trade thus diverts from the low-cost non-member country to the higher-cost partner country. The efficiency cost of trade diversion is $5 per ton multiplied by the number of tons initially imported into the domestic country.

The world of opera provides another—and novel—example of trade diversion. As reported by *Opera Magazine*, the Welsh National Opera recently engaged two American singers for the tenor and soprano roles in the opera *Rigoletto*. But to be able to perform in Britain, the two American singers had to receive a working permit, and an application for this has to be supported by British Actors' Equity Association. The working permit is not required of EEC artists coming to Great Britain, however, because EEC nationals are free to work in any country of the Community.

In the event, British Actors' Equity refused to support the applications of the two American singers. The result, however, was not the engagement of two British-born artists to replace them, but of two definitely less qualified Italian singers (less qualified than the American singers, that is). Trade diversion thus reduced the pleasure (economic well-being) of the audience at the *Rigoletto* performance. There was a substitution for a high-quality by a lower-quality source of supply induced by the Common Market rules (and British Equity). This is analogous to the substitution of higher-cost for a low-cost production in the usual definition of trade diversion.

The essential point of customs union analysis is that any "real world" customs union can be expected to be trade creating with respect to certain commodities and trade diverting with respect to others. The overall effect of the customs union on domestic economic well-being therefore is ambiguous. It will rise if trade creation outweighs trade diversion, and fall in the opposite circumstance. Naturally, the higher the common external tariff, the more likely that the customs union will decrease domestic economic welfare at fixed terms of trade. This is so because the higher the common external tariff, the greater the tariff disadvantage suffered by non-member goods vis-à-vis partner goods in the domestic market, and thus the greater the likelihood that trade will be diverted.

In addition to international trade, customs unions can divert the location of business enterprise in the world economy. Rather than be excluded by the common external tariff, non-member business firms can be protected by it by setting up business inside the customs union. The diversion of trade and the diversion of business firms have identical effects on resource allocation—each implies that the location of production shifts from a more to less efficient source. In the case described by Viner, resource misallocation occurs because international trade is diverted, while when business firms move from country to country, resource misallocation occurs because the location of business enterprise is diverted.

The case where a customs union leads to the diversion of business firms to the protected area raises an interesting point that is highly relevant to the issue of "free trade versus protectionism" as well as customs union. This is the *magnification* of the resource misallocation induced by a tariff when business firms can move from country to country. If business firms were specific to specific countries, the tariff would induce production of uneconomic amounts of the protected good by domestic firms only. This is the usual textbook example. But in an internationalized world of multinational corporations, the implicit subsidy rendered by the tariff to firms producing within the protected zone provides an incentive to foreign firms to produce there also. The effect is to increase the "coverage" of the tariff—i.e. the amount of *world* output of the good that benefits from the subsidy—and thus the resource misallocation induced by the tariff by comparison with the situation where business firms are not mobile. The tariff of the country that protects is "exported" to the rest of the world to the extent that the rest of the world sets up business in the protecting country. This "exporting" is undoubtedly a serious problem, since there is a good deal of evidence to suggest that American investment in Europe in the 1960's and foreign investment in the

United States in the 1970's has been related to an increase of protectionism in these areas.

The most important customs union between nation states in the world economy is the European Common Market, and Viner's theoretical work on customs union stimulated empirical economists to attempt to measure trade diversion and trade creation in the EEC. Williamson and Bottrill conclude that "intra-EEC trade in 1969 was something like 50 percent greater than it would have been if the EEC had not been created. Most of this rise appears to be attributable to trade creation rather than diversion. ..." [4] But while empirical economists have pictured the EEC as outward-looking and liberal, this view is not shared by everyone. The late Harry G. Johnson identified what he called "contemporary mercantilism" with the "pursuit of protectionist aims through the formation of supra-national trading blocks." He went on to add that "the European Economic Community represents the epitome of modernized mercantilism." [5] Though the beloved Professor Johnson was not immune from occasional over-statement, experience taught many of us who knew him well that to ignore his warnings was to court considerable peril.

Professor Johnson was a leading critic of the Common Agricultural Policy (CAP) of the EEC. The CAP supposedly is the EEC "customs union" for agricultural products. But it is a strange type of customs union—one that permits only trade diversion. The possibility for trade creation in the CAP is excluded, because the common price for agricultural goods inside the Community is determined not by the most-efficient producer in the community market, as a result of free competition, but by the least-efficient Community producer, as a result of the fact that the CAP authority sets prices inside the Community and sets them so high that even the least-efficient Community producer can stay in business. The common internal EEC price for agricultural goods gives the illusion of intra-union free trade but not the reality. The truth is that the CAP is not a customs union at all—merely a highly protectionist scheme to benefit Community producers at the expense of Community consumers and outsiders.

The customs union has been the most relevant exception to the most favored nation clause of GATT. There also were exceptions to the prohibitions of quantitative restrictions. GATT allowed contracting parties to apply quantitative import restrictions to deal with balance of payments deficits, to protect domestic agriculture under certain conditions and to promote economic development. Granted these are pretty large loopholes for clever lawyers to pass through. But experts feel that, notwithstanding these loopholes, GATT in fact did play an important role in the dismantling of quantitative restrictions in the post-War period.[6] It did this by establishing a commitment to a standard of conduct that could not be consistently controverted by the member states, and by providing a forum in which complaints could be aired.

Conclusion

In a well-functioning market economy, government interventions should be minimized other than for the provision of essential public services. There are, however, always special interests that want to alter the outcomes that result from the free interaction of buyers and sellers in the market place in their favor, and restrictions on international trade have been a favorite interventionist mechanism. Their popularity no doubt is due to the fact that their true purpose and effects are easily hidden behind the almost universal fear of foreigners, and the fact that foreigners do not vote in domestic elections. The slogan that it is foreigners who must pay, however false, has given trade restrictions considerable political appeal.

Tariffs and quotas have been imposed for all types of reasons: simply to raise tax revenue; to redistribute income to particular groups; to reduce unemployment; to improve the balance of payments; to accumulate gold; to promote an "infant industry"; and to prevent an older industry from dying.

Economists have consistently pointed out that trade restrictions are an inefficient means of achieving each of the above objectives. Trade restrictions are a poor way to raise tax revenue, a poor way to redistribute incomes, a poor way to promote domestic employment, and so on. The argument is that the overall economy suffers when the special interest is satisfied by the tariff or the quota. The group that gains income, gains employment, or gains gold does so at the expense of the overall community when the gain is achieved by a restriction on international trade. This argumentation is essentially one for efficient intervention. But behind this argument is the view often found that there should be no intervention at all, except when there is a true consensus for it in the community. "A deaf ear to special interest" is the true motto of the free trader.

The issue of free trade versus protectionism is that of the conflict between special interest and the public interest. It also concerns the preservation of the market economy and the price mechanism.

Free traders are against protection not only because it subordinates the general interest to special interest but because it is feared that protection will undermine the market economy and the price mechanism. Accordingly, free traders prefer certain types of trade restrictions to others. The tariff is felt to be a "conformable inter-ference." This exacerbates the conflict between free traders and protectionists, since the latter prefer the quota to the tariff; they believe the quota renders greater and more secure protection.

APPENDIX A

A FORMAL ANALYSIS OF THE TARIFF

The proposition that, at constant world prices, the tariff must reduce the economy's overall well-being or welfare is important enough to warrant demonstration. The argument can be presented most simply by means of a diagram. In Figure A.1, WS_W represents the world supply curve of a particular good. It indicates that at the given world price, OW, the country can import all of the good that it desires from abroad. How much of the good the country will in fact choose to import depends upon: (1) how much of the good the economy desires to consume at the given world price; and (2) how much of the good domestic producers desire to produce at the given world price. If at OW desired domestic consumption is greater than desired domestic production, the difference is imported from abroad.

The domestic supply curve is represented by S_dS_d in

Figure A.1. It shows the minimum price that domestic producers require to produce a given unit of the good in question. For example, to induce domestic producers to produce the Xth unit of the good, the minimum price they must receive is OW; to induce them to produce the X'th unit, OW' is the minimum price, and so on. The curve is depicted as rising from the lower left to the upper right to indicate the increasing costs of production.

The domestic demand curve, on the other hand, is depicted as falling from the upper left to the lower right. It shows the maximum price that the domestic consumer would be willing to pay for a given unit of the good in question in order not to lose from the purchase or exchange. For example, to consume the X''th unit, the maximum price the consumer is willing to pay is OW'. If he has to pay only OW—less than OW'—for the X''th unit, he gains WW' units of real income from the purchase. He therefore buys the X''th unit. If he had to pay more than OW' for the X''th unit, he will lose from buying the X''th unit and therefore does not make the purchase.

At the given world price OW, domestic production is WP and domestic consumption is WC. The difference, PC, is imported from abroad. This corresponds to the situation under free trade. Now, assume that the government imposes a tariff at the rate $W'W/OW$. Domestic prices rise to OW', while the world price remains constant at OW. The tariff creates a differential between the domestic price and world prices of the good in question.

Let us assume that the motive for the tariff is to raise the incomes of domestic producers of import substitutes. It can be seen in the figure that $WW'P'P$ equals the gain to domestic producers from the tariff. But while the tariff raises the price domestic producers receive for their good, it also raises the price domestic consumers must pay for it.

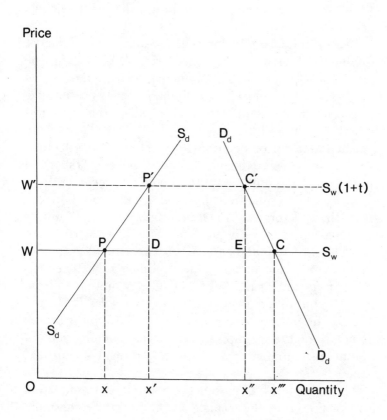

FIGURE A.1.

This imposes a loss upon domestic consumers equal to $WW'C'C$. That the domestic consumer loss ($WW'C'C$) *must* be greater than the domestic producer gain ($WW''P'P$) follows from the fact that domestic consumption must be greater than domestic production under free trade, since the case is, by definition, that of an import good.

If one considers only domestic consumers and domestic producers, the net loss from the tariff is $PP'C'C$. But the government also must be considered, and the tariff benefits the government. The government receives tariff revenue equal to the tariff rate multiplied by the cum-tariff quantity of imports.

The latter can be determined in the following manner. As a result of the higher domestic price of the good induced by the tariff, domestic production increases from P to P', while domestic consumption falls from C to C'. Both these factors tend to reduce imports—from PC under free trade to $P'C'$ with the tariff. Since $P'C'$ is the cum-tariff level of imports, and WW' (equal to $P'D$) the per unit tax on these imports, their product $DP'C'E$ equals the government's gain. When $DP'C'E$ is subtracted from $PP'C'C$, the difference is the sum of triangles $PP'D$ and $EC'C$. This difference represents the net loss to the overall economy, on the assumption that all the economic actors—consumers, producers, and the government—count the same.

The triangle $PP'D$ is sometimes called the production cost of the tariff, the triangle $EC'C$ the tariff's consumption cost. The production cost of the tariff relates to the fact that by increasing the price of the import good to domestic producers, the tariff induces a change in the location of production from a low-cost to a high-cost source. Domestic production of the import substitute increases by XX'. The total cost of producing XX'

domestically is $XPP'X'$, which is $PP'D$ greater than $XPDX'$, the cost of obtaining the XX' units from abroad. Thus, it is cheaper to produce the XX' units abroad and import them than to have these units produced at home.

The consumption cost of the tariff, on the other hand, relates to the fact that by increasing the price of the import good to domestic consumers, the tariff induces a reduction in the domestic consumption of the import good below its optimal level. The optimal level of consumption is that level which equates the good's marginal social value with its marginal social cost. This occurs at point C. At the lower level of domestic consumption, C', however, the marginal social value—indicated by $C'X''$—is greater than the marginal social cost—indicated by EX''. Social welfare would be increased by EC units of additional domestic consumption of the import good, but the distorted price system—that is, the price system distorted by the tariff—would prevent this. The tariff encourages the domestic consumer to consume too little of the import good by comparison with what the cost of such consumption would be.

The analysis of the tariff in Figure A.1 amply demonstrates the conflict between special interest and the public interest inherent in the issue of free trade versus protectionism. The tariff furthers the special interests of the domestic producers of import substitutes, but it does so at the expense of the economic interests of the overall community. Domestic producers of import substitutes gain $WW'P'P$, though the entire community loses the sum of $PP'D$ plus $EC'C$.

THE TARIFF VERSUS PRODUCTION SUBSIDY AS A REDISTRIBUTIVE MECHANISM

The superiority of the production subsidy by comparison with the tariff as a redistributive mechanism also can be demonstrated with the aid of Figure A.1. To transfer $WW'P'P$ amount of income to domestic producers of import substitutes with the tariff, the loss to the overall community (the efficiency loss) is the sum of the triangles $PP'D$ plus $EC'C$. There is both a production and a consumption cost to the redistribution. But to transfer the same amount of income to domestic producers by a production subsidy, there is only a production cost—the price of the import good to consumers remains the same.

To raise the price of the good by WW' to domestic producers, the government must spend $WW'P'D$—the per unit subsidy times the domestic output. This increases producer incomes by only $WW'P'P$, because the subsidy induces additional and high-cost domestic production in transferring the income. Note that if the domestic supply curve S_dS_d had been perfectly vertical, the increased price to producers would induce no additional domestic production, in which case the total outlay by government would be precisely equal to the domestic producer gain; there would be no production cost. Regardless, the production subsidy is a superior mechanism for redistributing income to producers than the tariff because the latter affects both consumer and producer prices, whereas only producer prices are affected by the subsidy. The difference between the two mechanisms becomes less important, however, as the domestic demand curve becomes more vertical. In the limit, when the demand curve is vertical, there is no efficiency difference between the two.

NOTES

1. Haberler comments on the equivalency argument. He writes: "Under given conditions of comparative cost of production and of demand and supply in the countries concerned it is always possible to find a duty equivalent to any given quota—that is to say, a duty which would restrict imports to the same level as the quota. It would, however, be a mistake to assume that the effects of a quota and an equivalent duty are the same." Gottfried Haberler, *Quantitative Trade Controls, Their Causes and Nature* (Geneva, League of Nations, 1943), p. 20.
2. I would like to thank Dr. Harry Grubert for bringing this argument to my attention.
3. Jacob Viner, *The Customs Union Issue* (New York: Carnegie Endowment For International Peace, 1950).
4. John Williamson and Anthony Bottrill, "The Impact of Customs Unions on Trade in Manufactures," *Oxford Economic Papers* (November 1971), pp. 323-351. Reprinted in Melvyn B. Krauss,

The Economics of Integration (London: George Allen and Unwin, 1973).

5. Harry G. Johnson, "Mercantilism: Past, Present, Future," in H. G. Johnson, ed., *The New Mercantilism* (Oxford: Basil Blackwell, 1974).

6. See, for example, Otto Hieronymi, *Economic Discrimination Against the United States in Western Europe* (Geneva: Librairie Droz, 1973), pp. 74–76.

CHAPTER II

THE NEW PROTECTIONISM

The "new protectionism," a term encountered with increasing frequency both in the media and in academic discussion, refers to an increase in the quantity of protectionism that is currently practiced in the international economy as well as to a difference in the form of protectionist measures. Both dimensions of the new protectionism—quantity and form—take as a standard of reference the international trading system envisaged by the General Agreement on Tariffs and Trade.

The GATT vision is that of an international system which consists of free enterprise market economies, based on the price system, linked to one another by unrestricted international economic exchange, whose governments seldom intervene in the private economy except when protectionist pressure becomes irresistible, in which case protection would be rendered by an instrument compatible with the workings of the market economy—namely, the nondiscriminatory tariff. The GATT vision never came to pass in its entirety. But it did have a profound effect in guiding the dismantling of the manifold controls that hampered international trade during the post–World War II period.

The New versus the Old Protectionism

In one sense, the new protectionism is not protectionism at all, at least not in the traditional sense of the term. The old protectionism referred exclusively to trade-restricting and trade-expanding devices, such as the tariff or export subsidy. The new protectionism is much broader than this; it includes interventions into foreign trade but is not limited to them. The new protectionism, in fact, refers to how the totality of government intervention into the private economy affects international trade. The emphasis on trade is still there—hence the term "protection." But what is new is the realization that virtually all government activity can affect international economic relations.

The emergence off the new protectionism in the Western world reflects the victory of the interventionist, or welfare, economy over the market economy. Jan Tumlir writes, "The old protectionism . . . co-existed, without any apparent intellectual difficulty, with the acceptance of the market as a national as well as international economic allocation and distribution mechanism—indeed, protectionists as well as (if not more than) free traders stood for *laissez faire*. Now, as in the 1930's, protectionism is an expression of a profound skepticism as to the ability of the market to allocate resources and distribute incomes to societies' satisfaction." [1]

It is precisely this profound skepticism of the market

economy that is responsible for the new protectionism. In a market economy, economic change of various colors implies reallocation of resources and redistribution of incomes. The consensus of opinion in many communities apparently is that such reallocations and redistributions often are not proper. Hence, the government intervenes to bring about a more desired result.

The victory of the welfare state is almost complete in northern Europe. In Sweden, Norway, Finland, Denmark, and the Netherlands, government intervention in almost all aspects of economic and social life is considered normal. In Great Britain this is only somewhat less true. Government traditionally has played a very active role in economic life in France and continues to do so. Only West Germany dares to go against the tide toward excessive interventionism in Western Europe. It also happens to be the most successful Western European economy.

The welfare state has made significant inroads in the United States as well as in Western Europe. Social security, unemployment insurance, minimum-wage laws, and rent control are by now traditional welfare state elements on the American scene. And, in its first year, the Carter administration proved particularly vulnerable to protectionists. Hardly an industry that asked the Carter administration for protectionist assistance had to walk away empty-handed.

The color television industry obtained "voluntary" export quotas. The steel industry has received subsidized loans and a reference price scheme. Sugar growers got higher prices for sugar and dairy farmers got higher prices for milk. The shoe industry got protection from foreign shoes and the trade unions got protection from illegal aliens. Under President Carter, the level of interventionism has accelerated at an alarming pace.

NOTES

1. Jan Tumlir, "The New Protectionism, Cartels and the International Order," in Ryan Amacher, ed., *Challenges to Liberal Economic Order* (Washington, D.C.: American Enterprise Institute, 1978).

CHAPTER III

THE INTERNATIONAL TRADE EFFECTS OF WELFARE STATE INTERVENTIONS

In referring to the welfare states of Western Europe, Harry Johnson has written that "in some countries, there now appears to be a commitment not only for every man to be employed, but for him to be employed in the occupation of his choice, in the location of his choice and, it would sometimes seem, at the income of his choice." [1] This is what the noted sociologist Daniel Bell calls the "revolution of rising entitlements." To attempt to meet these commitments, welfare state governments freely intervene into the private economy. These interventions can have significant effects on international exchange—not only on international trade in its narrow sense but on international capital movements and labor migrations as well. The purpose of this chapter is to analyze the international effects of welfare state interventions.

The range of intervention employed by the welfare states boggles the mind. There are labor subsidies, capital controls, cartel agreements, subsidized loans, regional developments grants, investment grants, price-fixing arrangements, production subsidies, consumption subsidies, export subsidies, tariffs, quotas, and so on. All these interventions—plus the tax structures of the economy—can significantly affect international trade. Not to be forgotten is that modern government, as a consumer of resources, has grown so large that it can dramatically affect trade patterns and flows. Finally, government can influence foreign trade in its role as an agency for redistributing income among different economic groups in the community.

Income Transfers and International Trade

The establishment of what may euphemistically be called an "equitable distribution of income" is an integral part of the modern welfare state. In reality, this term often serves as a cloak behind which the government carries out income transfers from the nonfavored to the favored group. The favored, it should be noted, may not be the poor. Rather, the new protectionism affects redistributions in accordance with the political and economic powers of certain "types" in the community.

Consider rent control, for example. Rent control redistributes income from landlords to tenants. But there is no reason to identify rich people with landlords and poor people with tenants. Indeed, the reverse is often the case. Tenants, being more numerous than landlords, have more votes. This fact may be the reason for rent control.

Much income redistribution in the welfare state is from capital to labor. Such redistribution can be expected to affect international trade in at least two ways: one direct and the other indirect. If one makes the traditional assumption that capitalists save a greater proportion of their income than laborers, overall savings can be expected to fall with the transfer of income from capital to labor. This implies less private investment and less investment *net* if government investment (or foreign investment) cannot make up the difference. The resulting decline in the growth rate leads to protectionist pressures to maintain domestic incomes and employment in weaker sectors of the economy.

A second, more direct implication for international trade of the redistribution of income from capital to labor relates to the different propensities of the two groups to consume (1) traded versus nontraded goods, and (2) exportables versus importables. If, given the constant price ratio between traded goods (considered as an aggregate) and nontraded goods (services), income redistribution increases the relative demand for nontraded goods, it can be said to increase the price of nontraded goods in terms of traded ones. This redistribution of income will increase both the consumption and the production of nontraded goods and decrease the consumption and production of traded ones in the economy. Since labor can be expected to have a higher marginal propensity to consume nontraded goods than capital (a major component of nontraded goods is government services), the often observed growth of the nontraded sector in the welfare states can be explained, at least in part, by the redistribution of income from capital to labor.

Income transfers from capital to labor can also affect the terms of trade between exportables and importables. If, at constant terms of trade, labor's marginal preference for imports, by comparison with exports, is greater than capital's, the redistribution may cause the terms of trade of the overall economy to deteriorate. On the other hand, the terms of trade can be expected to improve if labor's marginal preference for exports is greater than that of capital. But terms-of-trade effects, either an improvement or a deterioration, depend upon whether or not the country within which the income redistribution takes place is an important factor in international markets—the so-called big-country assumption. Otherwise, the internal redistribution will affect the *volume* of trade but will not affect the terms at which such trade takes place.

The terms of trade effect from internal income redistribution may not be of great importance to the *individual* welfare states of northern Europe—Sweden, the Netherlands, Norway, Denmark—which all are rather small countries. But this may not be the case for the welfare states taken as a *group*, since the relationship between capital's and labor's tastes will probably not vary substantially from country to country, nor will the direction of the income transfer in each state. If one is willing to accept the broad generalization that the northern European welfare states tend to export raw materials, sophisticated engineering products, and fuels, while they import food, semi-manufactured goods, and consumer goods—and at the same time assume that labor's marginal preference for the latter group of products is greater than that for the former group by comparison with capital's—then it can be argued that the internal income transfer policies of the welfare states have led to a deterioration in their terms of trade with the rest of the world. Income redistribution in this case can be said to reduce the size of the pie that is being redistributed.

Income Transfers and Guest Workers

Up to this point, the discussion has centered on how income redistribution affects international exchange. But the question can be transposed to ask how international exchange affects the ability of welfare states to redistribute income from capital to labor. That is, if the welfare state is heavily dependent on foreign labor, can income transfers from capital to labor be effectuated? The question is a relevant one, since the welfare state economies of northern Europe are big importers of so-called guest workers.[2]

The guest worker, or to-and-fro migrant, typically works in foreign countries for relatively short periods of time—say, six months to three years—to return home with the fruits of his labor abroad. He tends to live meagerly while in the "host" country in order to send or take home as much of his wages as possible. He produces income in the host country and consumes it in the home country.

Guest workers involve an international exchange transaction just as the export and import of physical commodities do. The home country exports labor services and receives labor remittances in return. The host country exports labor remittances for the import of labor services.

The export and import of labor services via guest workers is analogous to the export and import of physical commodities. This can be illustrated by a simple example. Italy exports shirts to Germany, the proceeds of which Italy can use to import German goods. Italy also exports guest workers to Germany, who work, for example, as street cleaners; this can be thought of as an export by Italy of street-cleaning services to Germany, the proceeds of which Italy also can use to import German goods. The two transactions are, in essence, equivalent.

Since guest workers can be thought of as but another

way in which countries trade with one another, the neoclassical idea of the "gains from trade" can be applied to the guest worker phenomenon. Both host and home countries can be presumed to benefit from the guest worker exchange transaction, just as both import and export countries can be presumed to gain from the international exchange of commodities. But there are important differences between the two.

Unlike straightforward commodity trade, the export of labor services implies that the "exporter" (the guest worker) must be present physically in the foreign country. While abroad, the guest worker pays taxes to, and receives social services from, the government of the host country. In effect, the domestic income redistribution and social service policies of the host country "spill over" to the guest worker, who, after all, is a citizen of another state—an outsider who has nothing to do with the internal social policies of the host country, but who by virtue of his temporary physical presence there enjoys an "undeserved" benefit or suffers an "undeserved" cost.

Assume that the social services the guest worker receives exceed the taxes he must pay to the host government. Since the situation of the guest worker vis-à-vis the host government is identical to that of the domestic worker, this assumption is consistent with that of an internal income redistribution program to benefit domestic labor. If the host country is a small one, as are most of the welfare states, it is a "price taker" rather than a "price maker." Thus, the wages paid to domestic workers is given by, and equal to, the wage in the world market, in the absence of controls on imported labor.

While guest workers can earn the world wage anywhere, in the host country they can earn the world wage plus the social surplus. If markets are competitive, the guest workers can be expected to compete for the social surplus offered by the host country by taking a lower wage than that offered elsewhere. Indeed, so long as the real income from the *sum* of the host country wage plus the social surplus is greater than that from the world wage alone, guest workers can be expected to bid down the host country wage. This process can be expected to go on until the real income from the sum of the host country wage plus social surplus is precisely equal to that of the world wage. After that it makes no sense for the guest workers to compete for the social surplus in the host country by accepting lower wages than are available in other countries.

Since it is the world wage that *determines* the domestic wage in the host country, and the domestic wage has been bid down by guest workers to gain the social surplus given by the host country government, the effect of extending the social surplus to guest workers is to frustrate the internal income redistribution program to domestic labor. The idea of this program is to increase the standard of living of domestic workers, by comparison with their initial situation, by giving them a social surplus. But the competition of guest workers for the social surplus reduces the domestic wage, so that domestic workers are no better off with the social surplus than without it. They receive the social surplus, of course, but they also receive a lower wage because of it. Guest workers also are no better off, for the same reason. The only ones to benefit from the social surplus to labor are the domestic *employers* of such labor, since the change has wrought a decrease in the wage they must pay.

One way to avoid this problem is to deny the net social surplus to foreign labor. Guest workers would not have to pay host country taxes but would have to pay (as much as administratively feasible, at least) for all social services received while in the host country. This policy, it should be noted, would run counter to Convention 143 of the International Labor Organization (ILO), which calls for equality of opportunity and treatment of migrant workers in several areas, including social security. But the standard for equality of treatment implicit in Convention 143 is based on the *location of production of income:* all workers producing income in the same country should be treated equally regardless of where that income is consumed. There would be no discrimination problem, however, if the standard for equality of treatment were based on the *location of consumption of income:* all workers consuming income in the same country should be treated equally regardless of where that income is produced. Since the foreign workers often produce income in the host country but consume it at home, if the standard of equality of treatment were based on the location-of-consumption precept, guest workers would prove less of a threat to domestic workers than when they receive the social surplus of the host country.

Today, this threat is handled in a different manner by welfare states. The social surplus is extended to all guest workers within the host country, but the number and type of guest workers are limited. In particular, some countries keep out guest workers with families or allow the guest worker to come in only if he leaves his family behind. The object of these strictures of course, is to reduce the social expenditure made by the host country on the guest worker. It seems clearly desirable to avoid enforced separation of families and to eliminate the spillover directly. Moreover, the elimination of quotas on guest workers would be a desirable development because it would prevent protectionist use of quotas to raise domestic wages to unnecessarily high levels.

In effect, guest workers represent two different types of threat to domestic workers. First, they bid the domestic wage down to get the social surplus. This problem has been discussed. But even in the absence of a social surplus guest workers tend to bring the domestic wage down to the level of the wage paid on international markets. Domestic employers gain and domestic employees (of identical quality to guest workers) lose by comparison with the situation where guest workers are completely excluded from the domestic country. This is a desirable development for the country that imports foreign labor. First, it can be shown that domestic employers gain more than domestic employees lose. Second, it allows economic growth and keeps labor costs competitive. Keeping labor costs artificially high by keeping foreign workers out is just as protectionist as allowing domestic wage claims to exceed productivity gains in an industry by keeping competitive imports out by a tariff (see Chapter I).

Guest workers are such an important part of the labor force in northern Europe that it is easy to overlook their significance to the U.S. economy. But guest workers are important in the United States as well, though here they often are referred to as illegal aliens because many enter the United States illegally. A better name for them would be "uninvited guests."

Let me give an example of an uninvited guest. It is a well-known fact that the price for household help has gone up considerably in major urban centers, for various reasons, including the generosity of welfare and unemployment benefits and the exclusion of foreign competitors. Why scrub floors when you can sit at home and enjoy the benefits of public largesse? Naturally those locals who are willing to scrub floors ask a high price. A friend of mine employs a very pleasant young woman from Latin America who is an illegal alien and whose price is closer to the world price than the inflated domestic price for domestic help. Both my friend and the woman from Latin America are satisfied with the arrangement, and why not! Both gain, and the attempt to charge unnecessarily high prices by local help has been thwarted.

On a national level, the AFL-CIO has worked very hard to keep illegal aliens out of this country. Their work bore fruit when President Carter announced his program to tighten up on illegal aliens, particularly those coming from Mexico. If successful, the program will have the dual effect of: (1) raising labor costs, particularly in the Southwest; and (2) cutting off an important source of income for our poorer neighbor to the south. In the press, illegal aliens are presented as posing a threat to American jobs. What they really threaten, of course, is the ability of American workers to obtain an unreasonably high wage.

Income Transfers and Capital Flight

The analysis of income transfers and guest workers raises the question as to whether some sort of analogous phenomenon can be expected to manifest itself with respect to income transfers and capital flight. Can the redistribution of income from capital to labor in a country be thwarted by capital flight?

The answer to this question is that so long as there is a market for the use of capital outside the country that seeks to reduce the real income of capital within its boundaries, the potential exists for capital to avoid the reduction in its real income if capital is free to move from one country to another. Consider a country that puts a tax on the income of capital that reduces its net rate of return below the world rate. But if capital were free to go abroad, the principal effect of this policy would be to *raise* capital's *gross* rate of return at home by precisely the amount that government sought to reduce the net return. This is so because internationally mobile capital always can earn the going rate of return to capital in foreign markets. Capital's domestic *net* rate of return must be equal to the foreign rate of return if there are no impediments to capital mobility; hence the effect of the tax on capital will be to raise capital's *gross* rate of return until it is sufficiently high to yield domestically employed capital a *net* return equal to the world return. Rather than taxing the *owners* of capital, the *users* of capital are burdened by the tax.

An example from the world of opera illustrates this point. The most mobile factor of production I know is the international opera star. He or she possesses a unique quality—unique "human capital"—that has the major opera houses throughout the world bidding for their services. Accordingly, when an international star, such as Luciano Pavarotti, comes to the Metropolitan Opera House in New York City and the U.S. government requires that he pay income tax on the income he earns at the Met (even though as a foreign resident he scantily benefits from U.S. public services), it can be expected that his fee to the Met will be raised to the extent of the taxes he must pay, or at least to the difference between the taxes he must pay here and those that he must pay abroad. The tax does not affect his net return (the net return to his "human capital")—it affects only the price that the Met must pay him. The government is taxing the Metropolitan Opera House, not Luciano Pavarotti, although formally Pavarotti sends in the tax money (on a high C, one presumes).

By making the international opera stars more expensive, the tax undoubtedly encourages the Met to hire them less often—and to use lesser singers instead. The result is a lower standard of performance and possibly a bigger deficit. If the percentage increase in the price of international stars is greater than the percentage decrease in the number of his appearances, the total deficit of the Opera House clearly rises. It has been written that the Metropolitan Opera House lacks a federal subsidy. But the situation is worse than that! An important "subsidy" the U.S. government can give the Metropolitan Opera is to stop taxing international opera stars.

An ironic perverse effect that taxing highly mobile capital can have is that labor can wind up paying the tax. It has been argued that a tax on capital to lower its net return will only increase its gross return if capital is internationally mobile. This increases the cost of capital to the users of capital. But business firms that employ capital may be able to shift this extra cost "backwards" onto labor if labor is "specific" to the industry that uses the taxed capital—that is, if labor cannot, for technical reasons, move from one industry to another. Because the industry must pay capital a higher rate of return, it pays labor a lower wage. Labor cannot escape this when it is, for one reason or another, "trapped" in a particular industry.

The point is that who finally pays the tax—the so-called question of tax incidence—is a highly complex matter, which depends to a large extent on which factor—labor or capital—has greater ability to escape the taxed sector or activity. It is for this reason that taxes on capital are often accompanied by controls on capital export. Without them, income transfer policies within interventionist states not only would be much less effective but could be perverse.

International Trade and the Government as a Consumer of Resources

In addition to its function of affecting income transfers from one private group to another, the welfare state government consumes substantial amounts of resources. For example, in Sweden in 1976, public sector consumption was one-half private consumption and 21 percent of total Swedish demand.

The transfer of resources from the private community to government can affect international trade in two ways. First, on the assumption that government does not discriminate between the domestic and the foreign sectors in its purchases, the transfer of income from the private to the public community works in a similar fashion to that of income transfers between different private groups. The transfer can affect the terms of trade, the volume of trade, and the size of the nontraded good sector, depending upon the marginal consumption preferences of the transferor and the transferee. But most governments do discriminate—and discriminate substantially—in their purchases in favor of domestic enterprise. Thus, how the transfer of resources from the private to the public sector affects the terms and volume of international trade and the size of the domestic nontraded goods sector depends upon two factors—the difference between the marginal consumption preferences of the private sector and government in the absence of discrimination, plus the discriminatory element in government purchases.

The literature has focused almost exclusively on the discriminatory element of government consumption. GATT's provisions are weak in this area. Reference is made to government purchases only in Article III 8(b) where it specifically excludes them from the basic non-discriminatory rule of the agreement.

With respect to practice, there is a great deal of difference between Europe and America. In the United States, discrimination is more open-based on the so-called Buy American Act of 1933. The Defense Department gives a 50 percent preference margin to domestic products. Other agencies give a 6 percent preference, or 12 percent on items produced by small businesses or firms. There is a considerable amount of open bidding for public contracts.

Other countries generally have few specific published regulations on government procurement. The use of open tender public procedures is uncommon, and most contracts are awarded on the basis of bids solicited from selected domestic suppliers or on the basis of private negotiations involving no competition. Many governments resort to administrative guidance to persuade purchasing entities to buy domestic products whenever possible. Charges of discrimination are hard to prove, since governments are seldom willing to reveal after the fact the considerations that rule in a contract award.[3]

Robert Baldwin has attempted to measure the protective effect of discriminatory government procurement policies in different countries by ascertaining their *tariff equivalent* in terms of import restriction. That is, a tariff of X percent would restrict imports to the same extent the discriminatory government procurement practices do. The methodology is quite simple. Baldwin compares actual government expenditures with a hypothetical figure that represents what government expenditures would have been in the absence of discrimination. His result, based on several simplifying though not unreasonable assumptions, is that the tariff equivalent of restrictive government procurement policies in the United States was 42 percent in 1958 and 43 percent in France in 1965—more or less the same. After a suitable warning about the crudeness of the data, Baldwin concludes that his "analyses . . . indicate that governments are more restrictive in their import policies than private purchasers." [4]

The argument that public consumption is more protectionist than private consumption implies that the more industries that fall within the purview of the public sector, the greater the overall level of protection in the economy. An interesting recent example of the dangers of public by comparison with private consumption relates to public television in the United States. To satisfy minority as well as majority tastes in America, public television coexists with commercial television. Many good things can be said about public television, but one sad one is that it is more susceptible to protectionist pressure than its private counterpart. When the Corporation for Public Broadcasting pledged federal funds to import a Shakespeare series produced in Britain by the BBC, the wrath of unions representing American performers and technicians was aroused. They objected to tax funds being used to finance any but American-made productions that employ their members. A *New York Times* editorial (February 12, 1978) argued that "The Federal Government has invested in public broadcasting not to subsidize domestic production or domestic labor but to bring the best available fare to viewers. More high-quality American-made shows are, of course, welcome; so are high-quality shows from Asia, Africa and anywhere else." But the fact remains that the threat of a ban on the British Shakespeare import could not be guaranteed until private corporations—a bank, an insurance company, and an oil company—agreed to fully underwrite the show—that is, until all public funds were fully withdrawn. One could not hope for a clearer example of the protectionist consequences of public consumption.

Government Procurement, Computers and Aircraft

Government procurement policies can be used to subsidize specific industries and even firms. An example where
a firm is subsidized by government procurement policy is
International Computers Ltd. (ICL) in the United
Kingdom.

The British computer industry is characterized by
competition between one large British firm—ICL—and
several American multinationals which have subsidiaries in
Britain. These include IBM, Burroughs, National Cash
Register (NCR), and Honeywell. There also are several
small British firms, such as British General Electric Corporation (GEC), Ferranti, Data General, and others that
operate in the market.

There are substantial subsidies to the British computer
industry from Her Majesty's Government. These are of
two types of subsidies—industrywide and firm-specific. All
firms that produce income inside Britain, regardless of
ownership, are entitled to the industrywide subsidies; this
means that American firms benefit as well as the British
firms. The sole beneficiary of the firm-specific subsidy,
however, is the British-owned ICL.

The two types of subsidy offered to the British computer industry reflect the twin objectives of government
policy in this area. The first objective is to encourage the
import of foreign advanced technology into Britain.
Hence, the industrywide subsidy. The second is to encourage the development of British-owned and -controlled
advanced technology. Hence, the firm-specific subsidy. It
should be noted that these objectives may be in conflict
with one another. Wedgewood Benn, former minister of
technology, writes:

There is a delicate balance which has to be struck. We need to provide a "sensible" amount of help for the indigenous company, but to avoid injury to the "good neighbour" policy towards American industry or alienation of the sources of advanced technology.

Benn continues:

As a regional Minister with responsibility for distribution of industry I am, in fact, through the highly discriminatory investment grant and other measures, encouraging firms, including many foreign firms, in the computer industry to come to this country and set up in business. Those United States owned computer companies who possess substantial manufacturing investment in development areas are among those who most resent preference to ICL. There is now a different distribution of ministerial responsibilities, and investment grants have been replaced by investment allowances, but the conflict of interest remains.[5]

It is clear that of the two types of subsidy—industrywide and firm-specific—the latter have been more controversial. ICL receives two types of firm-specific subsidies. From its inception in 1966 until 1977, ICL has received research-and-development grants from the government. But the main form of assistance ICL receives is related to government procurement policy. According to the U.K. Select Committee on Science and Technology, "the arrangements under which computers have been purchased for use in central Government . . . may be summarised as follows: to acquire from ICL large computers, and computers leading to them, using single tender procedures; to buy

smaller computers by single tender where necessary to
achieve compatibility; and in other cases to seek competitive tenders, but to allow preference in favour of any
British machine provided that there was no undue price
differential as compared with overseas suppliers."

Naturally, the American competitors of ICL in Britain
are anxious to remove the conflict between industrywide
and firm-specific subsidies by removing the firm-specific
subsidies, particularly the single-tender procedures. In
testimony before the Select Committee on Science and
Technology, Burroughs argued that "It was our hope that
H.M. Government in re-examining its policy would move
nearer towards acceptance of the contribution being made
by the British computer industry as a whole and recognize
the problems inherent in a single tender purchasing
policy." NCR emphasized the desirability of a strong and
healthy British computer industry and objected to the
identification of that industry with ICL.

The arguments of the American and British firms
obviously bore some fruit in that the 1971 Select Committee recommended to the U.K. government that "the
practice of 'single tender contract' should cease," though
"the Government continue to exercise a degree of preference in making its purchases." They also recommended
that "greater emphasis should be placed on direct support
for the industry by way of grants and development
contracts." These recommendations were rejected by the
U.K. government, however, and the single-tender contract
persists to this day.

The airplane industry provides another example of how
government purchases can subsidize firms and employment in the domestic country. British Airways is a
nationalized firm in the United Kingdom. Because it is a
"big buyer" of aircraft on the world market, British

Airways had substantial market power. And because it is a nationalized firm, it can use its market power to increase employment in Britain, by stipulating that the aircraft it purchases must be produced to some extent in the United Kingdom, and also can insist that the components of the aircraft—the engines for example—must be British-made. In 1978, the three American giants—Boeing, Lockheed and McDonnell Douglas—competed with a Franco-German consortium for providing British Airways with new aircraft. Boeing was the winner, but had to agree to use British-made Rolls Royce engines in the Boeing aircraft. If British Airways was a private firm, it could use its market power to get the best quality aircraft at the cheapest price, regardless of where the plane was produced. But the location of production is relevant precisely because British Airways is not a private firm. Production of aircraft engines in Britain is subsidized because British Airways is a nationalized firm. And, of course, it is the British taxpayer who pays for the inefficiency, since the cost of the aircraft to British Airways must be increased by comparison with the situation when the aircraft is built in the most-efficient location.

British subsidization of its computer and aircraft industries by government procurement practices is part of an overall pattern of subsidization, by some form or other, of advanced-technology industries—the aircraft, space, nuclear, and computer industries—by welfare states and market economies alike. For example, West Germany, which can be characterized as strongly noninterventionist, subsidizes all four industries mentioned above on the grounds that these industries are "key sectors of decisive significance for the whole of the economy." In the absence of reasonable criteria as to what constitutes a sector of decisive significance as compared with ordinary significance, this is a dangerous argument that can surely lead to protectionist abuse. No doubt protection of certain aspects of all of these industries can be defended under the auspices of national defense (though in this case there is the issue of "efficient" protection). But the suspicion remains that politicians have come to identify national prestige with advanced-technology industries—if not a false, at least a costly identification, many will argue—and that this more than national defense is the prime reason for their extensive subsidization.

Protectionism and Protection of the Environment

"The revolution of rising entitlements," as Daniel Bell notes, is "not just the claims of the minorities, the poor, or the disadvantaged; they are the claims of *all* groups in the society, claims for protection or rights." [6] One of these claims recently evidenced is that the government protect the "environment."

This is not the proper forum to discuss the merits or otherwise of whether and/or when the environment needs protecting. That subject warrants a book in itself, and indeed has been the subject of many. What is discussed, however, is how the protection of the environment often turns out in fact to be protection of domestic enterprise. The general point is that the more the government intervenes—for whatever motive—the greater the scope for intervention that discriminates against foreigners. The issue of landing rights for the Concorde in New York City is a case in point.

The granting of landing rights at Kennedy Airport in New York City for the Concorde was opposed by local citizens' groups who feared the supposed noise level of the supersonic airplane. Protection of American airplane manufacturers had nothing to do with their objections to the

Anglo-French plane. But the British and the French argued the case as a straightforward protectionist issue; to them the noise level or environment issue simply represented a convenient excuse for U.S. protectionists to hide behind.

The Concorde issue proved difficult precisely because the proposed ban in New York City had *both* protectionist and environmentalist aspects to it. Indeed, the Concorde dramatically brought to a head the question of whether *motive* is important if the *effect* of a policy measure is protectionist. The French and the British argued, in essence, that motive is unimportant—it is only the effect that counts. And one must agree! To make something as subjective as motive the prime requisite for determining whether or not a given policy measure is protectionist is to open the door to protectionist abuse.

For the environmentalist, protecting the environment without protecting local business enterprise means that, when warranted, environmental standards will have to be applied in an even-handed way to domestic and imported goods alike if such standards are to be acceptable to the *international community.* Such acceptability, of course, is important, since foreign retaliation against domestic environmental measures will serve to increase the *domestic* costs of these measures. For example, consider what the total consequences of imposing a ban on the Concorde in New York City would have been if the French and British had retaliated against the ban by imposing general restrictions on American imports.

Another example which illustrates how protection of the environment has meant protection of local enterprise is automobile safety standards in the United States. The entitlement here is to that of a "safe environment." It is a well-known fact that America has traditionally been a "big-car country," while Europe has tended toward the smaller car. With the emergence of the Organization of Petroleum Exporting Countries (OPEC) and the substantial increase in the price of gasoline, small cars have become more popular in the United States. But it seems that Detroit cannot build a small car that satisfies the U.S. consumer. The Italians, however, build a very popular small car (popular in Italy at least), the FIAT 500 and 600 models. These cars cannot be imported into the United States, though, because they are not considered to be safe by the U.S. government. This is very convenient for the Detroit auto manufacturers, which, judging from past experience, could not build a small car to compete with the FIAT 500. Of course, they argue that the lack of popularity of American-built small cars means that Americans do not want small cars in general, rather than that they just don't want the small cars that the Detroit manufacturers have offered them to this point (or is likely to offer them in the future, given that successful foreign-made small cars are kept out).

American safety standards for automobiles exemplify well the two guiding principles behind policies to maintain *national* product standards. The first is the chauvinistic one that the *quality* of domestic goods is superior to that of foreign goods. The second is that the consumer is too foolish to realize this and thus must be protected from his ignorance by the enlightened government—this being in direct contrast to traditional microeconomic theory, which assumes that consumers indeed are aware of quality differences and that should such differences exist between foreign and domestic goods, under reasonable competitive conditions they will be fully reflected in the prices at which the respective goods sell for in the marketplace.

Finally, while the example cited above is that of protectionist use of product standards in the United States, this practice is by no means limited to Americans.

Several examples in Europe can be cited. First, in the European Economic Community, rigid quality requirements govern wine imports. The French are "entitled" to good wine, which means French wine to the French government. Second, the EEC adjusts the price of its grain imports by arbitrary amounts that are alleged to reflect the "normal" difference in prices between the quality of the imported grain and the standard set for domestic grain—this under the banner that Europeans are entitled to good grain. Finally, in the Netherlands marketing regulations prohibit corn syrup as an additive for health reasons. Because the law applies to Dutch as well as to imported corn syrup, it appears innocent enough. But on closer examination the law on corn syrup effectively prohibits the importation of food products such as chocolate; fruit purees; pastes; most jams, jellies, marmalades, and so on, all of which contain corn syrup. This is because the Dutch appear to be the only people who are averse to corn syrup, which is cheaper than sugar. The reader may have noticed that these all are products for which Dutch producers are famous. The Dutch case is particularly interesting because it shows how even an apparently neutral environmental measure can turn out to be extremely discriminatory in fact—the wolf in sheep's clothes.

Labor Market Policies

One of the most mischievous arguments against free trade is that free trade creates unemployment. Let us investigate the source of this misunderstanding.

The argument for free trade assumes that the factors of production are mobile between industries and that factor prices are flexible. Critics of this argument respond that as (1) factor prices are not flexible and (2) factor resources are not likely to be mobile as between industries, free trade, by putting contractionary pressure on import-substitute industries, creates unemployment in these industries. A more sophisticated version of this argument is that flexible factor prices and factor mobility are likely only in the long run, and we all know that Keynes buried the long run some time ago when he noted that "in the long run we are all dead."

The implications of the argument against free trade on the grounds of the inflexibility of the domestic economy are quite startling. It means that changes in tastes be discouraged; that no new income transfer programs be started, since these would imply resource redirection; that economic growth be eliminated—in short, that *all change* be discouraged because the reallocation of resources implied by change cannot be effectuated by the economy without creating unemployment in the process. In effect, the argument is for a totally stagnant economy.

On the other hand, the "gains-from-trade" argument can be interpreted in a meaningful way as follows: that international trade gives the economy *the opportunity* to improve its aggregate economic position—an opportunity whose exploitation requires that factor resources be mobile and factor prices flexible. The argument for free trade, in other words, is an argument for flexible prices and internal factor mobility. Since the opportunities for mutually profitable trade always can be expected to be present, the theory warns us of the "costs" to the domestic economy of factor immobility and wage rigidity.

Of course, in the real world, factor prices are not always flexible, nor are factor resources always sufficiently mobile. What is the proper role of government in this situation? The answer depends on the cause of factor-price rigidity and factor immobility. If government action itself is the cause, then the government certainly should cease its unwelcomed and unproductive policies. On the other hand, if the cause lies in the private sector, there may be a role for government to promote flexibility and mobility by active intervention. The issue, in any event, is larger than just international trade. It relates to all changes in the economy, whatever their source.

One way the government can impede labor mobility, both occupational and geographic, is by social policies of extended unemployment benefits. The purpose of unemployment insurance is to help workers out during temporary periods of economic distress. But if unemployment insurance is available on an extended basis, as is the case in many welfare states, unemployment insurance *permits* the worker to resist the necessary adjustments that are called for by the economy. One such adjustment may be to leave the occupation in which he or she was previously employed. Another may be to leave the geographic area. Here, of course, there is a real conflict between the needs of a dynamic economy and the "revolution of rising entitlements." The economy dictates that the worker change occupations and/or location at the same time that the worker feels that he or she is "entitled" to work at his or her old trade at his or her old geographic location. More and more, workers have come to expect democratically elected governments to secure these entitlements for them—a trend that has already reduced the abilities of welfare economies to adjust to the needs of a changing economic environment.

Another government policy that restricts factor mobility and wage flexibility is the legitimization by government of labor-market monopoly practices. The restrictive practices of trade unions clearly constitute an ever increasing burden on the economies of the industrialized nations. In 1978, this is all too well known, and it is not only the outer reaches of the political right that are calling for reform in this area. Perhaps it is somewhat unorthodox to blame government for the growth of monopoly power in factor markets. But antitrust activity has traditionally been a legitimate function of government. It is clear that the time has come when governments must be a little more even-handed in the pursuit of their antitrust responsibilities. Monopoly practices in factor markets deserve attention that is at least equal to that given to monopoly practices in commodity markets.

Few governments pursue active policies to promote internal factor mobility. One exception is the so-called active labor market policy of Sweden. This policy was inspired by two trade union economists, Gösta Rehn and Rudolph Meidner. Rehn and Meidner argued that it was impossible to meet the unemployment problem in communities and regions suffering from structural contraction by *general* fiscal and monetary expansion. It would only lead to excess demand in the rest of the economy, Instead, they pleaded for selective measures to relieve distress in stricken areas while general economic policy should keep total demand within such limits that inflation could be contained. The function of government was to facilitate the movement of labor out of low-productivity uses into those with high productivity. Retraining, help in moving, and an intensive employment information service were the principle elements of the policy they recommended.[7]

Rehn and Meidner saw internal factor mobility as an integral part of *macroeconomic stabilization policy.* Assar Lindbeck writes that "two of Rehn's basic ideas . . . have been generally accepted: (1) that price stability is difficult to achieve if general excess demand for commodities and labor is not avoided; and (2) that the possibility of reconciling full employment and price stability is enhanced if the mobility of the factors of production is increased by a vigorous labor mobility policy."[8]

What have been the results of Sweden's experiment with an active labor market policy? One way to evaluate its effectiveness is to ask whether the costs to the taxpayers of the program have been greater or less than the gains to the economy from its ability to better adjust to changed circumstances. According to Göran Ohlin, "The impact of these measures is only now being submitted to serious study." But Ohlin is skeptical as to the effectiveness of the manpower policies. He writes, "In practice, the experience of active manpower policy in the 1960's showed that in spite of its great political appeal, it could not remove the hard-core problems of local contraction and stagnation . . . retraining which had been considered a quintessential element of active labor market policy, sometimes appears to have had no other effect than that trainees take jobs from others, and a tentative cost-benefit analysis has cast some doubts on the worthwhileness of those programs." [9]

Protection and "Adjustment Assistance"

Government policies whose objective is to improve the mobility of domestic factors of production are entitled to be called "adjustment assistance," since they aid the domestic economy in adapting to a changed economic environment. But a good deal of the present policies that go under the label of "adjustment assistance" have just the opposite intention. Rather than facilitate adjustment, their purpose is to impede it. In referring to trade adjustment assistance practices, Göran Ohlin noted: "adjustment assistance seems in practice often designed to bolster the defences against imports rather than clear the ground for them . . . few attempts have been made to accelerate the contraction of individual sectors." [10]

According to Caroline Miles, "an industry can be said to

have adjustment problems if the *speed of contraction* is such that the resources displaced are unable to find new employment within a reasonable period, or if there is a threat of significant and persistent employment." [11] GATT's Article XIX refers to "unforeseen developments" and the *rapid* changes of comparative advantage in the world economy which will cause situations in which *sudden* import increases put acute strain on individual sectors.

The emphasis on suddenness, rapidity, and speed should be noted. For the justification for trade adjustment assistance often has been to ease the speed of contraction to give the affected industry time to make an *orderly* retreat. At least, so goes the rhetoric! The reality, however, has been that rather than phase out sick industries, trade adjustment measures have tried to rejuvenate them.

The practical experience with adjustment measures in Europe has shown them to be little more than domestic subsidies of various kinds, justified on the pretense that they are necessary to ease the domestic adjustment to changed economic circumstances. Regional policies have been instituted on this basis. Grants are given to firms that scrap old plants, and subsidies are given to firms investing in new plants. Wage subsidies are given to "cover up" the real amount of unemployment in certain industries. In Europe, these practices often go under the name of the "new industrial policy." It is typical of the type of doublethink that goes on today that the European "reluctance to adjust" is fostered by policies that bear the title "adjustment assistance."

Adjustment assistance admirably demonstrates two important characteristics of the new protectionism. First is the "reluctance to adjust" on the part of the European economies. I take this to be a reflection of the "revolution of rising entitlements" in these countries—the people feel themselves entitled to certain economic amenities—so that adjustment that threatens these entitlements is resisted. In essence, what this phenomenon represents is an extension of political rights into the economic sphere. This cannot be done, of course, without substantial government intervention in the private economy.

Adjustment assistance programs also demonstrate the pursuit of protectionism in the name of free trade that has become common to the new protectionism. Being contracting parties to GATT, all the industrial nations are committed to the *principle* of free trade. But the reality of free trade is too much for them, given their domestic commitments, which often conflict with a liberal international order. Naturally, the domestic commitments dominate in the actual formulation of policy, but the principle of free trade is given lip service even if the policy directly contradicts the principles. This is because the mere mention of the principle is considered sufficient to keep one's internationalist credentials valid—and one gets away with it, of course, because everyone else is doing it.

In addition to adjustment assistance—a policy meant to impede adjustment—we have that divine French creation, "organized free trade"—a policy meant to impede free trade. What "organized free trade," or as it is alternatively referred to, "organized liberalism," means in plain English is cartel! Jan Tumlir writes that "there has occurred in Europe a surprising revival of the belief in the efficacy of cartels as instruments for solving the problems of adjustment and overcapacity." [12] What Tumlir finds surprising, in particular, is that "cartels have enjoyed more, and more open, official support than any of the cartels in the 1930's," especially since the "cartelization-rationalization movement of the interwar period was a disastrous failure."

A cartel, of course, is just the opposite of free trade. Producers conspire to determine a minimum price, and this price is enforced by producers who voluntarily agree to limit their exports. Tumlir reports that two industries in particular are seeking "to organize their free trade"—steel and shipbuilding. With respect to steel, the result has been the so-called Davignon Plan. According to the *Guardian* of London (November 7, 1977):

> The Davignon Plan ... has three main elements: An undertaking by the European and Japanese steel producers not to upset the American market with their exports, or to "compete unfairly" in other markets; an end to the campaign by the U.S. steel industry to get the Carter Administration—by way of the courts—to impose punitive anti-dumping duties on foreign steel imports; and coordinated steps to restructure the world steel industry including the phasing out of old plants and limits on the explosive growth of new steel-making capacity in Japan and many parts of the developing world.

Dumping

We all know what dumping is! Let me give an example from my youth. In my neighborhood there were many small ma-and-pa grocery stores. One day, with great fanfare, a link in a famous chain of supermarkets appeared on the scene. The local supermarket charged prices well below those charged elsewhere—in fact, cheaper than the supermarket itself charged in other stores. Naturally all the local housewives rushed to take advantage of the bargain prices. The other links in the chain financed this operation, whose purpose was to put the ma-and-pa grocery stores out of business. Once the competition was eliminated—for the family businesses did not have the financial wherewithal to meet the competition—the supermarket raised its prices to a level appropriate to its being the only grocery store in the neighborhood. The supermarket had successfully "dumped" upon my neighborhood.

Most people would agree that the supermarket is the villain of this piece. But let us consider a somewhat different scenario. Let everything remain the same except that now, after all the ma-and-pa groceries have been put out of business, the local supermarket, for some unexplainable reason, continues to charge lower prices than markets elsewhere. Let's assume that the supermarket in the local neighborhood charges prices below those in other markets forever. The ma-and-pa groceries may have cried "dumping," but the local housewives are grateful for this unexpected gift. The manager of the local supermarket has become the housewives' hero.

Imagine that you were given the power to prevent the local supermarket from selling cheaper than elsewhere. Would you use it? The ma-and-pa grocers undoubtedly would work hard to think up arguments why the entire neighborhood would benefit from preventing the supermarket from selling cheaper in their neighborhood than elsewhere. But the housewives would never forgive you. Is it worth it to make so many enemies for so few friends?

The answer might be yes if the few friends are powerful people in the neighborhood and the housewives could be fooled into believing that the supermarket was not sincere. For example, it could be argued that the supermarket really did intend to raise prices once the ma-and-pa stores were put out of business, even though this was not the case. The people who ran the supermarket could be depicted as outsiders who could not be trusted—not being neighborhood people like ma and pa.

It is interesting to note that under present GATT rules

both cases would be considered as dumping even though the economic effects of the two were vastly different. According to Article VII of GATT, dumping is defined as the sale of a product abroad at a lower price than is charged domestically. If that price difference is judged to cause material injury to an established domestic industry, that country may impose an antidumping duty to bring the price in the domestic market up to the price in the market of the exporting country. Since the supermarket chain charges different prices in different neighborhoods and ma-and-pa groceries suffer in both cases, antidumping measures would be taken regardless of whether or not the local supermarket intended to maintain a low-price policy in the local neighborhood.

The GATT rule seems unnecessarily biased in favor of domestic producers and against domestic consumers. It is not true that in every instance when a foreign country sells more cheaply in the world market than at home his intent is to put potential competitors out of business so that a monopoly position can be established. There is absolutely no evidence to suggest that Japanese firms that sell television and stereo sets in America cheaper than they do in Japan do this to put RCA and Zenith out of business to become monopolists in the American market. Charging different prices in different markets is rational profit-maximizing behavior, as is well known to students of price discrimination theory. It is a shame that domestic consumers are not allowed to benefit from price discrimination practiced by firms in foreign countries, just as it would have been a shame if the local housewives had been prevented from enjoying the benefits of price discrimination by the supermarket chain that charged cheaper prices in their neighborhood than elsewhere. The truth of the matter is that predatory dumping by foreigners in the

American market is much less of a problem than predatory protectionists who use alleged dumping by foreigners as an excuse to obtain protection in the domestic market.

Domestic Subsidies

One of the prime weapons welfare state governments employ to meet their manifold objectives is the domestic subsidy. The problem of defining domestic subsidies is not as straightforward as it may first appear to be. Alan Prest notes that "there is no neat and tidy single all-purpose definition" and argues that "the least unsatisfactory one is: payments which directly affect relative prices in the commercial sector, broadly defined." [13] The emphasis on *relative price*—the price of a good in terms of other goods—should be noted. If the effect of a subsidy is solely to affect *absolute price*—a proportionate change in the money prices of all goods—the subsidy can be expected to appreciate the country's currency. But across-the-board subsides will not disturb a preexisting efficient allocation of resources, since relative price is unchanged.

Domestic subsidies can be distinguished as being broad-based, intermediate-based, and narrow-based. The first applies to the economy as a whole, the second to specific industries and regions, and the last to individual firms and towns. Prest notes that "there has been a perceptible quickening of pace with narrow-base subsidies in recent years, especially since 1974." [14] The preferred form of narrow-based subsidies is the provision of capital by government at favored rates—whether by grant, loan, loan guarantee, or equity participation—usually in return for acceptance of government conditions on some key matters. It is precisely this aspect of the new protectionism that

Assar Lindbeck finds most objectionable. He writes that "many of the new selective interventions ... constitute a serious threat to the efficiency in the allocation of resources, perhaps even more so than the tariffs which have been removed, as tariffs often were more general types of interventions. From that point of view, it could reasonably be argued that future conferences on international trade should perhaps concentrate on reducing these various selective subsidies ... rather than cutting tariffs. *That would have the additional advantage of perhaps stopping, or even reversing, the enormous concentration of economic powers to centrally planned administrators and politicians, which is perhaps the major consequence for our societies of the even more selective interventions.*[15]

Three types of goods can be distinguished for purposes of our discussion: import goods, export goods, and nontraded goods. Subsidization of nontraded goods raises few problems, though by encouraging expansion of the nontraded good sector, subsidies do attract resources away from traded goods. There are problems, however, connected with domestic subsidies to export and import goods.

Consider the case of export goods—that is, goods for which at given world prices domestic consumption is less than domestic production. Just as export subsidies can be expected to increase exports, domestic subsidies to export goods also increase exports. But there is a significant difference between the two. Export subsidies discriminate between the domestic and the foreign sectors of the economy, whereas domestic subsidies do not: this is an important difference and explains why export subsidies for industrial goods (though not agricultural goods) are prohibited by GATT and domestic production subsidies are not.

GATT, however, is not silent on the subject of the trade

effects of domestic subsidies. Article III 8(b) specifically permits "the payment of subsidies exclusively to domestic producers." However, Article XVI of GATT directs each contracting party to notify the group as a whole if any of its subsidies operate directly or indirectly to increase its exports or decrease its imports. It then states: "In any case where it is determined that serious prejudice to the interests · of any other contracting party is caused or threatened by any such subsidization, the contracting party granting the subsidy shall, upon request, discuss with the other contracting party or parties concerned, or with the Contracting Parties, the possibility of limiting the subsidization." Under Article VI a country can also levy a countervailing duty if it determines that the effect of a domestic subsidy by another country is such as to cause or threaten to cause material injury to one of its industries or to an industry in some third country.

The difference between an export subsidy and a domestic production subsidy can be clearly demonstrated by a diagram. To put it simply, because it discriminates between the domestic and foreign sectors of the economy, the export subsidy creates a divergence between prices that prevail in the domestic market and those that prevail on world markets. The domestic production subsidy, on the other hand, does not discriminate between the two sectors, so that the domestic price continues to be equal to the external price.

The case of the export subsidy is shown in Figure 2. At the world price level OW (assumed to be given to the subsidizing country), the consumption point is C given the domestic demand curved DD and the production point is P given the domestic supply curve SS. WP production is reconciled with WC consumption by PC amount of exports.

An export subsidy increases the return from production

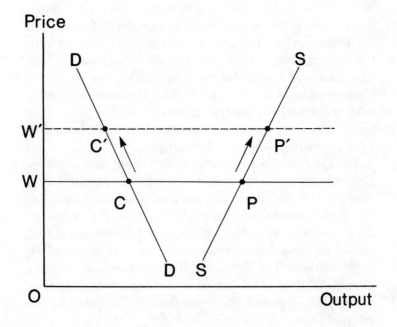

FIGURE 2.

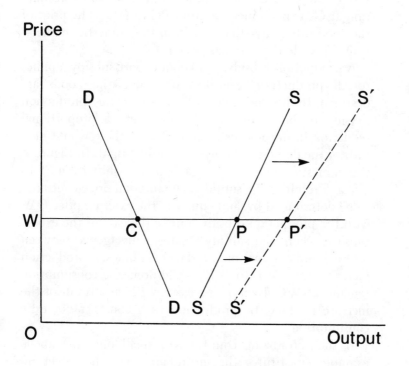

FIGURE 3.

for export by comparison with production for the home market. This stimulates producers to expand output up their supply curves, so that if the rate of subsidy is equal to $W'W/OW$, production increases from P to P'. Because the domestic supply curve is upward sloping, the price to domestic consumers also increases; hence consumption shifts from C to C'. With production at P' and consumption at C', exports increase from PC to $P'C'$. The price of the good internally—that is, within the domestic market—is OW', while the external price is OW.

A production subsidy, unlike an export subsidy, applies to all production regardless of where the goods are destined to be consumed. This allows the production subsidy to be treated *as if* there were a proportional reduction in output cost, in which case there would be a shift of the domestic supply curve to the right. In Figure 3, the domestic supply curve is assumed to shift from SS to $S'S'$ as a result of the subsidy. The internal price continues to be determined by, and equal to, the external price OW with the production subsidy (unlike the case of the export subsidy, where the subsidy creates a divergence between internal and external prices). Hence, domestic production increases from WP to WP', while domestic consumption remains at WC. Exports increase by PP' as a result of the increase in domestic production with constant domestic consumption.

If the subsidizing country is a small one, the above example constitutes the entire analysis. The effect on importing countries is considered to be too negligible to be considered. But if the subsidizing country is a large one in world markets, the effect of *both* the export subsidy and production susidy will be to turn the terms of trade *against* the subsidizing country. That is, at constant world prices, both the export and production subsidies increase the supply of the subsidizing country's export good on world markets. This increase must decrease the world price of the export good, which is a loss for the subsidizing country. The terms of trade—the price of a country's exports in terms of its imports—have deteriorated.

Naturally, when the world price of the subsidizing country's exports falls, consumers in the foreign (importing) country gain, and it can be shown that the foreign country, considered in net aggregate terms, also gains. But producers in the importing country lose, since foreign producers of import substitutes also receive a lower price for their products when its world price drops. Hence we have a reasonable motive for producers in the importing country to look askance at *both* export subsidies and domestic production subsidies in the exporting country. Furthermore, factors of production employed by the producers of import substitutes can be expected to share a viewpoint similar to that of the producers themselves.

From the common point of view of producers and factors of production employed in the sector that produces import substitutes, both the export subsidy and the production subsidy in the exporting country threaten the price of their product and thus their real incomes (this assumes the exporting country is a large one). But the export subsidy is worse, again because of the divergence it induces in internal and world prices. This divergence means that for equal *ad valorem* subsidization rates in the exporting country, the increase in exports on world markets will be greater with the export subsidy than with the production subsidy. This is so because the export subsidy induces a reduction in domestic consumption *as well as* an increase in domestic production, while the production subsidy induces only the latter. Hence, the export subsidy constitutes a greater threat to price on world markets than does the production subsidy in the exporting country.

To sum up, measured at constant world prices both the

production and export subsidies improve the economic position of *producers* in the subsidizing country, though both impose an efficiency distortion upon the economy. But if the subsidizing country is large in world markets, the gain from both types of subsidies to domestic producers is reduced because the world price of the export good (and thus the world price plus the subsidy) falls. Net, domestic producers of the export good can be expected to gain even if the world price falls, but the gain is not as great as it would be at a constant world price. The fall in the world price of the export good also hurts producers of this good in the importing countries, and their loss is unambiguous because they do not receive a subsidy, as do their counterparts in the exporting country.

From the combined view of producers and consumers in the importing and exporting countries, the fall in the world price of the export good of the subsidizing country represents a loss to the country of export and a gain to the country of import. This loss (a terms-of-trade loss) to the export country is in addition to the efficiency distortion of the subsidies measured at constant world price. Thus, the export country undergoes a double dose of welfare loss. The import country, on the other hand, enjoys an unambiguous welfare gain from the terms of trade improvement. The loss to producers there is less than the gain to consumers.

The discussion to this point has focused on subsidies to export goods. But subsidies also can be given to import goods, and these have consequences for international trade as well.

In the case of an import good, at the given world price OW in Figure 4, domestic consumption WC is greater than domestic production WP, the difference PC being equal to free trade imports. A production subsidy shifts the domestic supply curve to the right, from SS to S'S'. At constant world prices, this results in increased domestic production and a reduction of imports equal to *PP'*. Domestic consumption remains at *WC*, Hence, a production subsidy to the import good also can cause problems for *producers* of the import good in the foreign country, because it reduces imports. Indeed, if the country that gives the subsidy is a large one, the world price of the good can fall as a result of the subsidy.

The relation between the production subsidy to the import good and a tariff is analogous to that between the production subsidy to the export good and the export subsidy. The tariff causes the internal price of the import good to be greater than its external price. The tariff reduces imports because it induces both an increase in domestic production and a decrease in domestic consumption. With the production subsidy, on the other hand, the domestic price continues to be equal to the world price. But imports decrease because domestic production expands. Comparing an import tariff to a production subsidy of equal *ad valorem* rate, the tariff reduces imports to a greater extent because it affects domestic consumption as well as domestic production of the good. In Figure 4, the production subsidy reduces inputs by *PP'*, but the tariff imports by *PP'* plus *CC'*.

The U.S. government is becoming increasingly sensitive to the trade effects of industrial subsidies by foreign countries. They are considered to be "back-door" export subsidies and import duties. But this concern is largely misplaced. First, if the United States is a net importer of the good that is being subsidized by foreigners, not only do U.S. consumers gain, but they gain more than domestic producers lose from the foreign subsidies. Second, even if concern is only that U.S. producers do not "unfairly" suffer—and this is a poor guide for policy—it is not true that just because foreign producers receive subsidies and

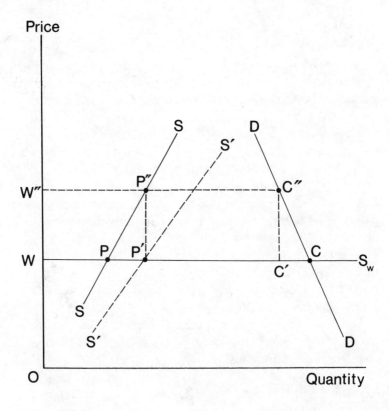

FIGURE 4.

U.S. producers do not that foreign producers are at an advantage vis-à-vis their American counterparts. This is because foreign competitors are often subject to constraints upon their behavior, imposed by government, while U.S. producers are free from such constraints. Thus, the advantage of industrial subsidies enjoyed by their foreign competitors is offset to some extent by restrictions on the firms' freedom to behave as they—the firms—see fit.

An example of this situation is the British Steel Corporation. British Steel is a nationalized firm and, as such, receives substantial subsidies from the U.K. government. This fact has been used by the American steel industry in its attempt to receive protection in this country. At first glance, the argument may look plausible: Is it fair to make steel producers in the United States compete with subsidized foreigners? But what is overlooked is that the British Steel Corporation has certain "social responsibilities" that American steel producers do not. For example, British Steel cannot buy coal on the free market; it must buy British coal. Furthermore, the freedom of British Steel to close a factory in one locale and open one in another place is severely restricted by government policy. In other words, British Steel can be forced to keep open factories in depressed areas to sustain employment in that area when it would be more profitable to shut the plant down.

British Steel suffers from a myriad of such cost-increasing interferences on its freedom of action that do not burden our industry. Whether the subsidies it receives from the British government are sufficient to compensate for these disadvantages or not is an open and empirical question. In terms of the diagrams that are used in this study, the domestic supply curve shifts to the *left* because of the cost-increasing interferences, and then shifts to the *right* because of the subsidies. Whether *net* the domestic supply curve shifts to the right or to the left as a consequence of government intervention involves an empirical analysis of each individual case.

The argument that the total effect of government intervention in an industry must be considered, and not just the subsidy element, has relevance to many of welfare state interventionist policies. Consider regional development grants, for example. These grants encourage firms to relocate in depressed areas. Such relocation, however, will impose extra costs upon the firm; if it didn't, the subsidy would not be necessary in the first place. Hence, the subsidy compensates for the excess cost of moving to the depressed area, so that the *net* subsidy to firms that relocate certainly is less than the subsidy itself. One must assume, though, that if firms do relocate in the depressed area they must receive some subsidy. Furthermore, the regional grants benefit firms that are willing to operate in the depressed area without a subsidy. For these firms there is no extra cost element imposed upon the firms, and the subsidy is pure gain.

The case where the government imposes an extra cost on the firm or industry and then gives a compensatory subsidy should be distinguished from that where an industry or firm finds itself in deep trouble because of inefficiency or labor troubles and the government helps the firm with a subsidy. A good example of the latter is the situation of the Chrysler Corporation in the United Kingdom. After several unprofitable years there, Chrysler Corporation let it be known that unless some subsidy was forthcoming from the British government it would cease production operations in the United Kingdom. To prevent this, the British government made a potential financial commitment to Chrysler of £162.5 million ($320 million). The government's commitment of £162.5 million comprises £72.5 million to meet possible losses, a £55 million loan for capital expenditure, and a guarantee for other borrowing of £35 million. These commitments, it should be noted, were given at a time when Chrysler could not obtain funds through normal procedures, so that the subsidy element in them is quite large.

The Chrysler situation represents a case where the domestic supply curve has shifted to the left because of increased labor costs in the United Kingdom, and not because of a government-imposed social commitment. The subsidies compensate for this by shifting the curve to the right. But even if the subsidy had not been forthcoming, it is doubtful whether the supply of Chrysler cars on the *world* market would have decreased. Production simply would shift from the United Kingdom to some other country, and the U.K. market would be serviced from abroad. The U.K. government was willing to pay a subsidy to keep Chrysler's production facilities in the United Kingdom because it didn't want to deal with the unemployment that a Chrysler pullout clearly would have implied. The subsidy represented a transfer from British taxpayers to Chrysler workers (who caused the supply curve to shift to the left by obtaining wage increases greater than productivity gains) at a constant level of employment. But the international effects of this transfer were minimal, just as the international effects of domestic subsidies are minimal when they compensate for a cost-increasing social commitment imposed on firms by government.

The Export Subsidy Issue

Export subsidies can be applied either to all export industries or to selected ones. Unlike a general production subsidy that does not affect comparative advantage and can be efficiently adjusted for by an appreciation of the currency of the subsidizing country, currency appreciation cannot efficiently adjust for a general export subsidy. This is because the general export subsidy alters relative price. Too much of the export good and too little of all other goods are produced because of a general export subsidy.

Selective export subsidies are often used to give economic assistance to particular industries. In this sense, they are similar to industrial subsidies. But, as previously noted, export subsidies discriminate between the domestic and foreign sectors of the economy, whereas industrial subsidies do not. Because of this, the GATT rules concerning export subsidies are much stricter than those concerning industrial subsidies.

Article XVI of GATT specifically condemns the use of export subsidies. It directs all members to "cease to grant either directly or indirectly any form of subsidy on the export of any product other than a primary product which subsidy results in the sale of such product for export at a price lower than the comparable price charged for the like product to buyers in the domestic market." Note that the prohibition of export subsidies relates solely to industrial goods.

Since the developed countries (excluding South Africa and Australia) put into effect the GATT provision banning export subsidies on nonprimary goods, government aid to exporters of industrial commodities has been largely indirect. Liberal tax deductions for expenditures associated with developing overseas markets and the availability of export financing at concessionary rates through government-controlled financial institutions are the methods most frequently employed to boost export sales. Consider, for example, the so-called DISC (Domestic International Sales Corporation) program in the United States.

The corporation income tax applies to income earned in

all lines of corporate endeavor in the United States. But according to the DISC legislation, income earned in export-related activities is deferred from corporate taxation for a certain number of years. This is clearly an export subsidy, since the deferred tax can be invested to earn the going interest rate. Furthermore, inflation insures that when the tax finally is paid, the real value of the tax—that is, the value of the tax in terms of goods and services—will be less than when the liability is incurred. DISC is a good example of an indirect export subsidy that is applied via the tax code. Domestic transactions are taxed in one way, while export transactions are taxed in another more favorable way.

Robert Baldwin, in describing a second type of indirect export subsidy, reports that "most governments of the industrialized countries currently subsidize the export-financing process. Subsidization usually consists of establishing special financing or refinancing facilities as well as providing favorable insurance and guarantee arrangements for credit granted by private institutions. Both types of help enable exporters and foreign importers to obtain credit at interest rates lower than those in financing comparable domestic transactions." [16]

The practices that are generally considered as export subsidies by the seventeen nations that signed the GATT declaration to prohibit export subsidies on industrial goods in 1960 are:

1. Currency retention schemes or any similar practices which involve a bonus on exports or re-exports;
2. The provision by governments of direct subsidies to exporters;
3. The remission, calculated in relation to exports, of direct taxes or social welfare charges on industrial or commercial enterprises;

4. The exemption, in respect of exported goods, of charges or taxes, other than charges in connection with importation or indirect taxes levied at one or several stages on the same goods if sold for internal consumption; or the payment, in respect of exported goods, of amounts exceeding those effectively levied at one or several stages on these goods in the form of indirect taxes or of charges in connection with importation or in both forms;

5. In respect of deliveries by governments or governmental agencies of imported raw materials for export business on different terms than for domestic business, the charging of prices below world prices;

6. In respect of government export credit guarantees, the charging of premiums at rates which are manifestly inadequate to cover the long-term operating costs and losses of the credit insurance institutions;

7. The grant by governments (or special institutions controlled by governments) of export credits at rates below those which they have to pay in order to obtain the funds so employed;

8. The government bearing all or part of the costs incurred by exporters in obtaining credit.

The prohibition of industrial export subsidies by GATT undoubtedly is related to the feeling that the pursuit of special interest in one country should not negatively affect the economic position of foreigners. But GATT's concern for the effect of an export subsidy (or domestic subsidy) on foreigners seems to be misplaced. According to Harry Johnson, "export subsidization has its main effect ... in increasing the welfare of foreign consumers at the expense of the domestic taxpayers who pay the cost of the subsidy." [17]

GATT's concern with the effect that the pursuit of

domestic special interest has on foreigners stands in direct contrast to classical comparative cost theory. GATT fears that the promotion of a domestic gain by an export subsidy will entail a foreign loss. International trade theory tells us that the export subsidy imposes a loss upon the subsidizing country but renders a gain to foreigners. The paradox is resolved once it is realized that GATT's concern is with domestic and foreign *producers'* special interests, while trade theory refers to the welfare of domestic and foreign *consumers*.

This difference in emphasis—on consumers and on producers—serves to remind us that GATT is, above all, a political document. Though its vision of a liberal international economic order is based upon economic consumer-satisfying precepts, its function of defining acceptable and nonacceptable behavior in international commercial relations is necessarily political. That is, the governments of the contracting parties must agree to the standards of behavior set out by GATT if they are to abide by them. Export subsidies (by others) traditionally have been viewed by businessmen and government officials as a particularly unfair means of (foreign) government intervention—by comparison to tariffs, for example—though economists have not been loath to note that the imposition of tariffs by foreigners can be just as prejudicial to domestic producers as foreign export subsidies.

Students of GATT have pointed out and, to some extent, have been puzzled by GATT's asymmetrical attitude toward tariffs and export subsidies. Baldwin writes, "Each type of distortion is deemed undesirable but export subsidies more so than import duties."[18] The reason for this asymmetrical attitude can be traced to postwar American commercial policy interests. For one, there is the American-inspired free market emphasis of GATT and the related preference for the tariff as the mechanism of trade control. Second, the tariff was considered to be an important part of the European reconstruction effort within a regional framework, which the United States supported. On the other hand, the United States—reversing its earlier opposition to strict rules on export subsidies because of our own substantial use of agricultural export subsidies—supported bans on export subsidies in the mid-1950s because of both their increased incidence in Europe and lessened use in the United States. It should be noted that present U.S. trade policy seeks more comparable treatment between agricultural and industrial products, particularly since some of the principal present subsidy problems relate to agriculture—that is, EEC use of agricultural export subsidies.

Export Subsidies and Countervailing Duties

GATT is an institution that sets standards of acceptable modes of behavior in international commercial relations, but it has no way to enforce these standards. Enforcement is left to the contracting parties themselves, and the threat of retaliation by the aggrieved party is the prime enforcement mechanism.

In the United States, the deterrent to alleged unfair subsidy practices abroad is the countervailing duty. The relevant U.S. legislation concerning countervailing duties is the Tariff Act of 1930 (Sec. 303[a.I]):

Whenever any country . . . or corporation shall pay or bestow, directly or indirectly, any *bounty* or *grant* upon the manufacture or production or export of any article or merchandise manufactured or produced in such country . . . , any such article or merchandise is dutiable under the provisions of this Act, then upon the importations of any such article or merchandise into the United States, . . . , there shall be levied and paid, in all cases, in addition to the duties otherwise imposed by the Act, an additional duty equal to the net amount of such bounty or grant, however the same be paid or bestowed.

The countervailing duty, as its name implies, is conceived to be a "defensive" instrument. Its primary function is to insure that other nations do not engage in unfair trade practices. But the problem with the countervailing duty is that what is fair or not is left to the judgment—the unilateral judgment—of the alleged aggrieved party. The U.S. legislation, for instance, is sufficiently broad to enable what in theory is a defensive weapon to be, in fact, a menacing and intimidating "offensive" weapon. In the wrong hands, the countervailing duty can be a devious protectionist device—a wolf dressed in sheep's clothes.

Nowhere is this point made clearer than by the recent situation in the United States where two major U.S. corporations—U.S. Steel and Zenith Electronics—have taken the U.S. Treasury to court to force the Treasury to impose countervailing duties against foreign competitors because of the foreign practice of rebating the sales tax upon export. The export tax rebates are alleged to be bounties and/or grants under the provisions of the Tariff Act—this in spite of the fact that such export tax rebates are perfectly legal under the GATT rules. Article IV(4) of the GATT reads as follows:

No product of the territory of any contracting party imported into the territory of any other contracting party shall be subject to anti-dumping or countervailing duty by reason of the exemption of such product from duties or taxes borne by the like product when destined for consumption in the country of origin or exportation, or by reason of the refund of such duties or taxes.

The economics of the so-called border-tax-adjustments issue are clear. Economists such as James Meade, Harry Johnson, Gary Hufbauer, and the present author all agree that it is not legitimate to equate export tax rebates with export subsidies. The tax rebate helps equalize the conditions of competition between countries by removing a potential tax disadvantage from the exports of the tax-imposing country. An export subsidy, on the other hand, distorts the conditions of competition by giving the exports of the subsidy-giving country a fiscal advantage in world markets. One, in fact, is the opposite of the other.[19]

Unfortunately, economics may not be the deciding factor when the U.S. Supreme Court reviews the Zenith case in late spring of 1978. The courts already have ruled in several instances that the rebate of excise or sales tax upon the export of merchandise by foreign countries does indeed constitute a bounty or grant under the Tariff Act. The most recent instance was in *American Express Company* v. *United States,* but this ruling goes back to 1903 in *Downs* v. *United States* when the courts sustained the imposition of a countervailing duty on sugar exported from Russia on which excise taxes (imposed on all sugar produced in Russia) had been remitted. This interpretation was later upheld in *F. W. Meyers and Co.* v. *United States* (1903) and in *Nicholas and Co.* v. *United States* (1919). It is not clear whether the Supreme Court in the Zenith case will take a different view of the matter.

In the event that the Supreme Court rules in Zenith's favor, the U.S. Treasury will be compelled to countervail against the Japanese export tax rebate. Ironically, the long-run losers in a Zenith victory may not be the Japanese producers. The erection of a tariff wall around the American electronics industry will only encourage foreign firms to tunnel under the wall by building plants and factories in this country. The losers will be American consumers, who will have to pay higher prices, and American firms and workers in export industries, who will suffer from foreign retaliation. And retaliation is a virtual certainty, since the imposition of countervailing duties to offset export tax rebates constitutes a clear-cut violation of GATT rules.

What is particularly worrisome about a Zenith victory in the U.S. Supreme Court is the possibility that it may lead to a full-scale trade war. A suit by U.S. Steel to compel the Treasury to countervail against European specialty steel products because they allegedly benefit from a rebate of value-added tax upon export is now on the New York Customs Court agenda. And since the value-added tax is widely used in Europe, and rebated on exports, many other industries can be expected to press the Treasury in a similar fashion.

The issue of the export tax rate and whether or not it constitutes an export subsidy is a clear example of how the countervailing duty can be used as an "offensive" protectionist device. The essence of the problem is that it is up to the country in question alone to determine what is a fair or an unfair foreign-trading practice, and its judgment is final, regardless of the fact that it may be in contravention of sound economic principles and international agreement, as in the Zenith case. The so-called aggrieved party is judge, jury, and executioner—a situation that invites protectionist abuse.

NOTES

1. Foreword by Harry G. Johnson to G. Denton, S. O'Cleireacian and S. Ash, *Trade Effects of Public Subsidies to Private Enterprise* (London: Trade Policy Research Centre, 1975), p. xiii.
2. The analysis of this section is based upon M. B. Krauss and W. J. Baumol, "Guest Workers and Income Transfer Programs Financed by Host Governments," *Kyklos* (forthcoming).
3. Committee on Ways and Means U.S. House of Representatives, *Briefing Materials Prepared . . . On the Subject of Foreign Trade and Tariffs* (Washington, D.C.: U.S. government Printing Office, 1973), p. 57.
4. Robert Baldwin, *Nontariff Distortion of International Trade* (Washington D.C.: The Brookings Institution, 1970), p. 77.
5. *The Prospects for the U.K. Computer Industry in the 1970's* (Fourth Report of the Select Committee on Science and Technology, Session 1970–71, H.C. 621), p. xxxviii.
6. Daniel Bell, "The Public Household—On 'Fiscal Sociology and the Liberal Society,' " *The Public Interest* (Fall 1974), p. 39.
7. Göran Ohlin, "Adjustment Assistance in Sweden," *Adjustment for Trade* (Paris: Development Center of the OECD, 1975).
8. Assar Lindbeck, *Swedish Economic Policy* (Berkeley: University of California Press, 1974), p. 41.
9. Ohlin, op. cit., p. 208.
10. Ohlin, op. cit., p. 9.
11. Caroline Miles, "Adjustment Assistance Policies: A Survey," *Adjustment for Trade*, p. 17.
12. Jan Tumlir, op. cit., p. 3.
13. A. R. Prest, "The Economic Rationale of Subsidies to Industry," in Alan Whiting, ed., *The Economics of Industrial Subsidies* (London: Her Majesty's Stationary Office, 1976), p. 65.
14. *Ibid.*, p. 66.
15. Assar Lindbeck, "Economic Dependence and Interdependence in the Industrialized World," *Marshall Plan Commemoration Conference*, Château de la Muette, Paris, June 2–3, 1977, p. 16 (Krauss's italics).
16. Robert Baldwin, op. cit., p. 52.
17. Foreword by Harry G. Johnson to Denton, O'Cleireacain and Ash, op. cit., p. xxxiii.
18. Baldwin, op. cit., p. 46.
19. Melvyn B. Krauss, "How to Avoid a Trade War," *Challenge Magazine* (July–August 1977).

CHAPTER IV

THE PROBLEM OF WORLD TAX AND SUBSIDY HARMONIZATION

At first glance, the coexistence of the welfare state and the free market in different parts of the world economy would appear to entail few problems. The welfare state goes its way—the same for the free market. But the situation is not so simple.

"To each his own" would be fine if both types of economies were not linked to one another by international trade and by the fact that both capital and labor can move from country to country. But they are linked. The welfare states of northern Europe—Sweden, Norway, Denmark, the Netherlands, and Great Britain—all are small and exceedingly open economies. The ratio of traded goods to total GNP is quite high. Indeed, it may be argued that the development of the welfare state in these small open economies is due precisely to the economic insecurity that being a "price taker" with a large traded-goods sector necessarily implies. They are extremely vulnerable to changes that occur in the world outside them.

The linkage between the welfare state and free market economies provided by international economic exchange of various forms creates pressures for the "integrity" of each of the two economies. These problems are of two types—subsidy harmonization and tax harmonization. The subsidy harmonization problem for free market economies is how to respond to substantial subsidization of enterprise in the welfare state without becoming a welfare state itself. The tax harmonization problem for the welfare state is how to respond to lower rates in the market economy without becoming less of a welfare state.

International Subsidy Harmonization

The substantial subsidization of domestic enterprise by the welfare states creates pressures on the free market economies to similarly intervene, because free market goods compete with welfare state goods in the international marketplace. It should be mentioned at the outset that the extent to which this is a real problem, and not just an excuse for protection in free market economies, is when the foreign subsidies are not just compensation for an inefficiency "imposed" by the welfare state upon their local enterprise but a *net* subsidy, in the sense that the fiscal advantage enjoyed by foreign firms is greater than any inefficiency imposed on them by their welfare governments. When there is a net subsidy, what type of problem do they present for the market economy?

As already noted, foreign subsidies that reduce the price of the subsidized good on world markets involves a gain for domestic consumers of the good and a loss for domestic producers of like goods. Whether domestic consumers gain more or less than domestic producers lose depends upon whether the domestic country is a net exporter or importer of the subsidized good *in world markets*. If a net exporter, domestic producers lose more than domestic consumers gain, so that net the domestic economy loses from foreign subsidization. But if a net importer, domestic consumers gain more than domestic producers lose, so that net the domestic economy gains.

Regardless of whether the domestic economy gains or loses from the foreign subsidy, domestic producers can be expected to claim that the "foreign gift" to domestic consumers is not fair—to them, that is—and argue that they should receive a similar gift from the domestic government. In effect, domestic producers will argue for a "global harmonization" of subsidies. This translates as, "we subsidize our producers because foreign governments subsidize theirs." The free market adjusts to the welfare state and becomes more like the welfare state in the process.

The conflict between the welfare state and free market economies is clear if global harmonization is defined as commensurate treatment for domestic producers in all parts of the globe. If the standards of the free market economy adjust to those of the welfare state, then the integrity of the free market is undermined. If those of the welfare state adjust to the free market, then it is the integrity of the welfare state that is undermined. The pressure, of course, is on the free market to adjust to the welfare state, because it is free market goods that are at a competitive disadvantage.

There are essentially two solutions to the problem of the global harmonization of subsidies as defined above— supranationalistic and nationalistic! The supranationalistic solution is a reform of GATT to give this international body judicial powers and enforcement facilities to decide the rights and wrongs of subsidization disputes. Whether there is a legitimate cause for concern, and what remedial measures should be taken when an abuse is determined, would be decided by a disinterested body of international experts, and not by organized vested interests. Moreover, penalties could be levied on an international basis, not just by the injured party. Possibly the threat of internationalized retaliation would be sufficient inducement for the offender to cease and desist. One would be less than honest to note, however, that there is virtually no chance that such a reform of GATT could take place. There is insufficient political will.

The nationalistic and preferred solution is that government hold steadfast in maintaining the integrity of its preferred economic system. Surrender to the desires of free market producers for "global equity" means adopting foreign conceptions as to what is right rather than following one's own course. Even if the losses to domestic producers from foreign subsidization is greater than the gains to domestic consumers, the net loss to the free market economy can be considered as a "cost" that is well worth paying for maintaining the integrity of its preferred economic system. Indeed there need be no cost at all if the efficiency of domestic enterprise is not as it should be, and the foreign subsidies induce domestic firms to be more efficient in their efforts to compete on international markets against the subsidized goods.

International Tax Harmonization

It is well known that the overall tax burden is much greater in the welfare state than in market economies. In 1974, tax revenue as a percentage of GNP was 47 percent, 45 percent, 44 percent, and 45 percent in the welfare states of Denmark, Norway, Sweden, and the Netherlands, respectively, while in Germany this ratio was 38 percent and in the United States it was 29 percent. In 1977, the ratio rose to over 50 percent in Sweden.

The international tax harmonization problem raised by this difference in tax burden between the two types of economies is how the welfare state should respond to the incentives that its citizens have to emigrate to the low-tax country without becoming a market economy in the process. That is, how does the welfare state retain its integrity and at the same time avoid the emigration of its productive citizens?

Some of the problems related to differences in the levels of taxation of capital already have been discussed in Chapter III. The point made there was that controls on capital exports could be expected in welfare states to effectuate their demonstrated preference for redistributing income from capital to labor. There could also be expected to be controls on labor importation for the same reason.

One type of capital export that is difficult to control, even for the welfare state, is the export of "human capital"—that is, highly productive skilled citizens. This is one significant difference between the welfare states, which are democracies, and the Eastern European bloc, which refuses to allow its citizens to emigrate freely.

The issue of the effect of high tax levels and the emigration of skilled individuals from welfare states is a complex one. First, it should be pointed out that it is not only taxes that are relevant. In judging whether to emigrate or not, the welfare state citizen must consider the subsidies he or she receives from the government as well. Thus, while emigration may appear to be clearly advantageous if only tax-level differences between the welfare state and market economy are considered, it can appear to be less so when subsidy differences also are taken into account.

Next, it must be noted that it is not sufficient to consider only differences in *net* taxation between the welfare state and free market economies. When one leaves the welfare state, one is also leaving a particular country. The citizen may despise the welfare state but love the country which houses it.

Each country consists of a bundle of characteristics that cannot be found elsewhere. When one emigrates, one trades the bundle of characteristics of one country for the bundle of another. Since, on the whole, the bundle of characteristics of the "country of emigration" is likely to be worth more than that of the "country of immigration" to the potential migrant (though when the migrant leaves for political or religious reasons, this will not be the case), the welfare state citizen can be expected to emigrate only if the value of the difference in net of tax income between the two countries is greater than the value of the difference from trading bundles of national characteristics. Naturally, the more similar the countries of emigration and immigration, the more important the net taxation factor will be. One reason Englishmen tend to migrate and Swedes do not is that the English were very successful in spreading their culture and language throughout the world, while the Swedish experience is very unique.

The foregoing assumes that the income-earning potential for the welfare state citizen is certain in both the welfare state and market economies. But there is a risk factor that also must be considered in the "to move or not to move" calculus. What the potential migrant usually must compare is a more certain income profile in the welfare state with a less certain income profile in the market economy. Risk takers are more likely to emigrate than those who are risk adverse. This means that, by and large, young people are more likely to be migrants than old ones.

The record shows that there has been no major migration from the welfare states of northern Europe despite high taxes. If one considers only *net* taxation, this is likely to be negative mainly for talented high-productivity persons. Being talented, such persons learn how to "adapt" to their environment. There are always loopholes, and evasion is quite common. One favorite loophole is to work abroad for a few years. If these are high-productivity years, one can build up a nice tax-free or, at least, lightly taxed nest egg there. The idea is to spend as much as possible of your high-productivity years in the market economy where taxation is light and as much of your low-productivity years in the welfare state where subsidization is heavy.

Another reason why highly taxed, highly talented people do not leave the welfare state is that their skills may be country-specific. This would be the case of the lawyer, but not the dentist. Yet another may be the restrictive practices of the market economy. It may be difficult for a foreigner to get a license to practice medicine or dentistry in the country of immigration. Finally, it is easier to be an important person in a small country like Sweden, Holland, Denmark, and Norway than it is in a large one like the United States. Many prefer to be a big fish in a small pond to the alternative and are willing to pay for it.

Consumption versus Production Taxes

A further tax harmonization problem in the world economy relates to the fact that the European countries rely heavily on *consumption taxes* to finance their public sectors, while *production taxes* are favored in the United States. Examples of U.S. production taxes are the corporation income tax and the employer's social security tax. An example of European consumption tax is the value-added tax.

To put the issue in its most simple form, a domestic consumption tax exempts exports from the tax because exports are not consumed domestically. A domestic production tax, on the other hand, taxes exports because exports are produced domestically. Thus, if one country uses one type of tax and the other the other type, the exports of the country that employs the production tax will be disadvantaged in world markets by comparison with the country that uses the consumption tax, provided that the taxes in both countries are not general taxes.

If, however, both countries employ general taxes, the exports of the country that employs the production tax will suffer no disadvantage. This is because the country imposing the general consumption tax either will support this tax by destination principle border-tax adjustments—import compensatory duties combined with export tax rebates imposed at the same rate as that applied to the domestic tax—or the currency exchange rate between the two countries will adjust to take into account the difference in tax-induced absolute price levels in the two countries.

Assume Europe imposes a general consumption tax—that is, an equal *ad valorem* tax on all goods and services—while America imposes a general production tax. In Europe, the absolute consumer price level rises in proportion to the tax if Europe's monetary authority allows the money supply to sufficiently increase. Because America's consumer price level is constant, the rise in consumer prices in Europe will move Europe's balance of payments toward a deficit vis-à-vis America unless: (1) there is a regime of flexible exchange rates, in which case Europe's currency depreciates vis-à-vis America's currency, or (2) Europe supports its general consumption tax by destination principle border-tax adjustments, in which case no exchange rate change will take place. Border-tax adjustments combine import compensatory duties and export tax rebates imposed at the same *ad valorem* rate as the increase in Europe's consumer prices. For example, if Europe's consumer price level rises by 10 percent because of the tax, then the border-tax adjustments must be imposed at a rate of 10 percent. Currency exchange rate depreciation and destination principle border-tax adjustments are perfect substitutes for one another, at least so far as the balance of trade is concerned.[1]

It has sometimes been argued that the increased flexibility of the currency exchange rate in the present international monetary system has rendered moot the trade problems associated with different tax regimes in Europe and America. But this would be true only if production taxes in the United States and consumption taxes abroad were truly general. This most certainly is not the case, at least with respect to the U.S. corporation income tax. American businessmen who complain that U.S. exports do not compete on equal terms with foreign goods in world markets are correct. But it is not, as often charged, because of unfair export subsidy practices abroad. Rather, it is because the United States uses production taxes to finance the public sector and Europe uses consumption taxes.

One way for the United States to remove the tax disadvantage suffered by exports in world markets is to copy its foreign rivals and make sure the domestic taxes also are passed forward to consumers. To accomplish this, like our partners, America must tax imports at the same rate as that with which domestically produced goods are burdened and exempt exports from the domestic tax. These border-tax adjustments would insure that U.S. domestic taxes would not burden U.S. exports.

There are two ways in which the United States could introduce border-tax adjustments—that is, convert its domestic taxes from production to consumption taxes. One way is to apply border-tax adjustments to the present corporation income tax, in which case the prices that corporate producers receive for their goods, and the prices that consumers pay for them, will be proportionately increased. The other way is to replace the corporate tax with a European-style value-added tax.

The United States thus faces a difficult choice. If our preferred system of tax imposition is to be maintained, we must reconcile ourselves to the fact that our exports will continue to be at a disadvantage in world markets. To remove the disadvantage, we must adopt the tax practices preferred by our trading partners. The choice is ours, so to speak, because the tax pressure in the international economy is on our exports and not theirs.

It may be argued that our freedom to make this choice is limited, at least with respect to applying border-tax adjustments to our present corporation income tax. This is because the present GATT rules allow border-tax adjustments only for so-called indirect taxes. They are prohibited for direct taxes. Kenneth Dam summarizes GATT's position on border-tax adjustments: "When upon exports of goods the exporting state refunds indirect taxes previously paid upon goods, no problem of violation of the export subsidy provisions of Article XVI arises. Nor does any problem arise in the case of exemption from such taxes of goods destined for export. This conclusion follows from the principle that the exemption of an exported product from duties or taxes borne by like product when destined for domestic consumption, or the remission of such taxes in amounts not in excess of those which have accrued, shall not be deemed to be a subsidy."

This dispensation from the subsidy rules is not considered, however, to extend to direct taxes, such as corporate income taxes. Refunds of direct taxes on exports therefore not only fall under the export subsidy provisions of Article XVI but also give rise to a right on behalf of any importing country suffering injury to impose countervailing duties under Article IV.

It should be noted that GATT's asymmetrical attitude toward the imposition of border-tax adjustments—allowing them for indirect taxes, prohibiting them for direct taxes—has no basis whatsoever in economic theory. It is based on the naive assumption that only indirect taxes are reflected in the prices of goods and services. But who could seriously argue that the corporation income tax does not affect the prices of corporate goods. Certainly not public finance specialists who have argued this question for the past fifteen years. The GATT rule should be changed to allow border-tax adjustments for all taxes!

Given that a change in the GATT rules is not likely to occur in the immediate furture, the tax harmonization conflict between Europe and America can be resolved by U.S. adoption of a European-style value-added tax. Public finance experts such as A. C. Harberger have long argued the merits of substituting the value-added tax for this country's corporation income tax, and more recently, commentators have argued that the value-added tax replace the U.S. social security tax as well.[2] Substituting a value-added tax for *both* the corporation income tax and the social security tax would introduce a sufficient amount of generality into the U.S. tax structure as to render moot the international trade effects of the different tax regimes.

It also can be argued that from the purely domestic point of view, the introduction of greater generality into the tax structure would be a good thing.

NOTES

1. See H. G. Johnson and M. B. Krauss, "Border Taxes, Border Tax Adjustments, Comparative Advantage and the Balance of Payments," *Canadian Journal of Economics* (November 1970), pp. 595–602.
2. A. C. Harberger, "A Federal Tax on Value Added," *The Taxpayers's Stake in Tax Reform* (Washington, D.C.: Chamber of Commerce of the United States, 1968). Also see David Wilson, "VAT Only Solution to SS Funding Mess," *Boston Globe*, February 27, 1978.

CHAPTER V

STAGNATION AND THE WELFARE STATE

The great attraction of the welfare state to many persons is that it appears to combine high rates of economic growth with high rates of social consumption—that is, economic affluence with social justice to boot. This is because the basic relationship between economic growth and social consumption is viewed to be complementary. The higher the rate of economic growth, the greater the potential social consumption.

Economic growth is conceived to *allow* social consumption without creating strains on the society. Daniel Bell writes, "economic growth has been a 'political solvent.' While growth invariably raises expectations, the means for the financing of social welfare expenditures ... without reallocating income ... or burdening the poor ... has come essentially from economic growth. ... As the Kennedy and Johnson administrations found out ... the

Congress was more willing to vote for the social welfare costs of the New Frontier or the Great Society so long as economic growth provided additional fiscal revenues, than to reform the tax structure or increase the weight of taxes in the society." [1]

The argument of this chapter is that Bell's analysis is seriously incomplete. While economic growth may permit social consumption in the short run, in the longer run social consumption will reduce economic growth. The thesis is that the true relationship between economic growth and social consumption is competitive—that is, that there exists a trade-off between economic growth and social consumption. High rates of economic growth are thus conceived to be incompatible with high levels of social consumption.

One reason for this incompatibility is that high levels of social consumption necessarily imply protectionist measures that stagnate the economy. The new protectionism did not develop in a vacuum. It is an outgrowth of social policies that promise economic security—that labor and capital be kept in low-productivity uses where they are comfortable rather than being forced to adjust to alternative high-productivity uses. High rates of social consumption must stagnate the economy by making the economy rigid and inflexible. The new protectionism represents the means by which *rigor mortis oikonomikus* sets in.

The Inherent Contradictions of the Welfare State

It is novel to write about the inherent contradictions of the welfare state. Usually it is capitalism that is alleged to be the victim of an inherent contradition. The Marxist view, if one sentence can do it justice, is that because of "inherent contradictions" large imbalances between production and consumption will make the demise of capitalism inevitable. This position has been modified, as I understand it. We now have a neo-Marxist and even a neo-neo-Marxist interpretation, as well as, one might add, reasonably flourishing capitalism in some parts of the globe. I am sure I will be forgiven if I "usurp" the inherent-contradictions theme and give it something of a new twist.

Simply stated, the inherent contradiction of the welfare state is that the welfare state requires a high level of productivity to support it, but that welfare state interventionist policies necessarily reduce productivity levels. Hence, it is argued, the welfare state is not a sustainable phenomenon in the long run. It consists of policies that undermine the factors upon which it critically depends.

Consider, for example, the case of Sweden. Since the industrialization process started in Sweden in 1870, the Scandinavian country had a good overall growth record. In the pre–World War II period, it grew somewhat faster than in the other OECD countries, while in the postwar period it grew somewhat more slowly. Since the modern welfare state in Sweden did not begin until after the war (although the Social Democratic party first came to power in 1932), Sweden's growth record by comparison with that of other OECD countries should serve as a warning to those who would argue that Sweden is wealthy because it is a welfare state. Rather, the reverse is true. Sweden has a welfare state because it is wealthy.

The ascension of Social Democratic parties in the politics of northern Europe and of the Democratic party in the United States can be interpreted as a reflection of an increased demand for *economic security* on the part of populations with steadily rising incomes. This increased demand—the "revolution of rising entitlements"—can be taken to mean the *right* of workers to a job, at the location

of their choice, and at the income of their choice. Assar
Lindbeck notes that during the postwar period one
characteristic feature of economic policy in the Western
world has been the increase in the *number* of policy
targets. This is true not only in the northern European
countries but in the United States as well. No longer do
governments just aim for full employment; they also aim
for satisfactory distributions of employment among regions, sexes, and races.

To meet its expanded commitments, the government
makes extensive intervention, through the kinds of protectionist devices discussed, into the private economy. Since
the industries and jobs that are threatened by a changing
economic environment can be expected to be weak
industries, fulfillment of the welfare state commitments
usually means keeping resources in low-productivity and
out of high-productivity uses. Protection of the shipbuilding, shoe, steel, and textile industries are examples of what
economic security implies. The essential point is that the
welfare economy becomes increasingly unable to adjust to
a constantly changing environment because its social
commitments prevent it from doing so. The result must be
stagnation.

Disincentives to produce are inherent in the welfare
economy. The commitment of the welfare government to
provide economic security "from the cradle to the grave"
cuts the link between production and consumption for
welfare state citizens. The enjoyment of economic resources becomes unrelated to economic performance.
Naturally, production suffers when both employers and
employees know the state will bail them out no matter
how poorly they perform.

Some of the disincentives to produce are planned;
others are unintended by-products of welfare policies.
Planned disincentives to produce are exemplified by

programs that encourage workers to take an increasing proportion of their incomes in the form of leisure. The four-day week and work rules that make sick leave too much of a temptation for many to resist are examples. On the other hand, the fact that leisure represents tax-free income in countries where marginal tax rates on work income are high—sometimes astronomically so—means that the increased demand for leisure also is an unintended by-product of other social policies. The increased demand for leisure in welfare states is reinforced by the fact that while taxes are positively related to work income, subsidies either are negatively related to work income or are not related to work income at all. It thus cannot be argued that by taking increased leisure the citizen of the welfare economy reduces the subsidies he receives as well as the taxes he must pay. In fact, the opposite is the case. Taxes are reduced and subsidies are probably increased as more leisure is consumed.

The increased demand for leisure is one of the major consequences of high taxes in welfare states. But there are other consequences that also tend to stagnate the economy of the welfare state. The increased demand for leisure is a form of tax avoidance. Another such form is the use of barter as a substitute for monetary transactions. The local dentist in a welfare state may not accept cash for his services. But he will accept the services of the person who needs dental work, because the exchange of services for services cannot be taxed. The point is that it is easier to hide services received in kind than cash from the tax collector. The consequences of the increased use of barter is reduced efficiency in the economy, since the efficiencies created by the use of money as a medium of exchange are lost.

There is, of course, a great deal of tax avoidance in the welfare economy. That is how many citizens come to live with high tax rates. But the danger of tax avoidance is that it can divert resources from more important to less important economic uses. Since resources respond to net of tax rather than to gross of tax returns, they flow where the net of tax return is highest. But this can very well be to a use that has less economic value than its alternatives. The result is a tax-induced misallocation of resources. The alternative that appears most profitable to the private person is not the most profitable for the community as a whole, because the tax differentials have given the private person the wrong signals.

The emphasis on economic security in welfare states undoubtedly has led to the demand that income (and economic power in general) be redistributed from capital to labor. The consequences of such redistribution on economic growth can be summarized as follows:

1. Reduce savings if the savings propensity of capitalists is greater than that of labor;
2. Increase the demand for leisure;
3. Encourage resources to stay in low-productivity and out of high-productivity uses;
4. Encourage capital flight, which can be prevented only by efficiency-distorting controls;
5. Increase the demand of foreign labor to work in the welfare state, which can create efficiency distortions;
6. Encourage the flight of "human capital"—that is, the exit of talented high-productivity citizens;
7. Encourage tax avoidance.

Regardless of whether one feels the redistribution of income from capital to labor to be equitable, the consequence of such redistribution surely is to undermine the national product which finances social consumption in the welfare state.

This has become a subject of some concern in Europe and America. Will there be sufficient output ten years hence to finance the pension I am paying for today? This concern reflects a certain skepticism about the younger generation by their elders. By establishing the government as an intermediary between different generations, the welfare state did not take the fate of the older generation out of the hands of the young, as some mistakenly thought. Indeed, the opposite may be the case, since a good deal of social expenditure in the welfare state consists in trading present for future consumption. If future product is insufficient to support the claims on it—including those of the older generation to pensions and the like—there is going to be one large group of disappointed Danes, Dutchmen, Swedes—and Americans—some ten to fifteen years from now. The current crisis of the U.S. social security system bears witness to this problem.

Interestingly enough, in the northern European welfare states, the decrease in productivity levels induced by the welfare state policies has not occurred as rapidly as some might have expected. This is because the older generation of northern Europeans, raised in a competitive atmosphere, had the work ethic sufficiently instilled in them to resist the welfare state incentives to slow down and do less. However, the consistent attacks on individualism and the competitive spirit, which starts in the schools at an early age, along with the promise of guaranteed economic security, have made their mark on the new generation of northern Europeans. The old values have been undermined, including the Protestant religious values that were compatible with hard work and saving; productivity is down; and the welfare state is threatened for the first time in northern Europe. To put this point in the technical jargon of the economist, the "elasticity of response" to the welfare economy's "disincentives to produce" appears to be greater with the younger generation than with the older one. This should serve as a stern warning to those who would make "competition and individualism" dirty words in the United States.

One important implication of the enhanced response to the welfare economy's disincentives to produce is the present inflation that affects most of the developed world. The welfare economy does little to constrain the desire to consume—indeed, it enhances it by redistributing income from savers to consumers—at the same time that it dampens both the desire to produce and efficient production. The inevitable result is inflation. The inflation that appears to be built in to the developed economies would be reduced if the restriction on production imposed by production taxes, social changes, minimum wages, and income taxes were removed. It also could be expected to be reduced if resources which are kept in comfortable low-productivity uses were transferred to high-productivity ones.

The thesis that high levels of social consumption restrict economic growth is supported by Charles Kindleberger's argument as to the cause of Europe's outstanding growth record during the 1950s.[2] Kindleberger attributed Europe's outstanding growth record to the fact that northern Europe had available to it during the 1950s virtually limitless supplies of labor at reasonable rates—in economist's technical jargon, a perfectly elastic supply curve of labor. Once started, growth could gather momentum because the increased demand for labor implied by growth would not bid wages up.

Eventually, of course, rapid economic growth in northern Europe would exhaust the supply of labor available to it at a fixed wage. At this point, wages could be expected to rise as the North and the South competed for the increasingly scarce labor. Economic growth in the North would then slow down. But this would be a result of a natural economic process and not the outcome of an artificially imposed increase in the price of labor imposed by government. The word "artificial" is used because the increase in the cost of labor to firms would not be the result of labor's scarcity but of its political power to extract income transfers from the rest of the community.

Minimum wages, social security taxes, the encouragement by government of monopolistic practices by trade unions are all part of the welfare economy, and all contribute to making the cost of labor to firms higher than the free market for labor services would dictate in their absence. It is no accident that the increased incidence of social changes to make labor artificially expensive on the one hand, and a dramatic slowdown in the growth rates of the Western economies by comparison with their growth performance in the 1950s and early 1960s on the other, have occurred almost simultaneously from the late 1960s to the present. And while correlation does not prove cause and effect, it certainly doesn't disprove it either.

The analysis of the preceding paragraph argues that the cause of the "stagflation"—inflation with sluggish growth—that presently afflicts the Western economies can be laid at the doorstep of the welfare state interventions in America and northern Europe that have made labor an artificially costly factor of production at the expense of capital. Stagflation has been the undesired though omnipresent by-product of alleged socially just income redistribution policies. The long-run implications of this is that the welfare state is self-destructive. It both depends upon economic growth and destroys it. In the long run, the demand for a secure economic income at a given level or rate of increase, regardless of the changes that are being wrought elsewhere, proves illusory because the attempt to obtain the secure income reduces the ability of the economy to continue to produce it. It is perhaps the essential irony of the welfare state that the attempt to insure one's economic position serves only to insure the opposite!

NOTES

1. Daniel Bell, "The Public Household—On Fiscal Sociology and the Liberal Society," *The Public Interest* (Fall 1974), p. 43.
2. Charles P. Kindleberger, *Europe's Postwar Growth* (Cambridge, Mass.: Harvard University Press, 1967).

INDEX OF NAMES

INDEX OF TOPICS

117